**THE PUBLIC
MAPPING
PROJECT**

McCourtney Institute for Democracy

The Pennsylvania State University's McCourtney Institute for Democracy (http://democracyinstitute.la.psu.edu) was founded in 2012 as an interdisciplinary center for research, teaching, and outreach on democracy. The institute coordinates innovative programs and projects in collaboration with the Center for American Political Responsiveness and the Center for Democratic Deliberation.

Laurence and Lynne Brown Democracy Medal

The Laurence and Lynne Brown Democracy Medal recognizes outstanding individuals, groups, and organizations that produce exception innovations to further democracy in the United States or around the world. In even-numbered years, the medal spotlights practical innovations, such as new institutions, laws, technologies, or movements that advance the cause of democracy. Awards given in odd-numbered years highlight advances in democratic theory that enrich philosophical conceptions of democracy or empirical models of democratic behavior, institutions, or systems.

THE PUBLIC MAPPING PROJECT

HOW PUBLIC PARTICIPATION CAN REVOLUTIONIZE REDISTRICTING

MICHAEL P. MCDONALD AND MICAH ALTMAN

CORNELL SELECTS

An imprint of
CORNELL UNIVERSITY PRESS
Ithaca and London

Cornell Selects, *an imprint of Cornell University Press, provides a forum for advancing provocative ideas and fresh viewpoints through outstanding digital and print publications. Longer than an article and shorter than a book, titles published under this imprint explore a diverse range of topics in a clear and concise format— one designed to appeal to any reader. Cornell Selects publications continue the Press's long tradition of supporting high quality scholarship and sharing it with the wider community, promoting a culture of broad inquiry that is a vital aspect of the mission of Cornell University.*

Open access edition funded by the McCourtney Institute for Democracy at Pennsylvania State University.

First published 2018 by Cornell University Press

Printed in the United States of America

Library of Congress Cataloging-in-Publication Data
Names: Altman, Micah, author. | McDonald, Michael, 1967– author.
Title: The public mapping project : how public participation can
    revolutionize redistricting / Micah Altman and Michael P. McDonald.
Description: Ithaca : Cornell Selects, an imprint of Cornell
    University Press, 2018. | Includes bibliographical references and index.
Identifiers: LCCN 2018038389 (print) | LCCN 2018039938 (ebook) |
    ISBN 9781501738555 (pdf) | ISBN 9781501738562 (epub/mobi) |
    ISBN 9781501738548 | ISBN 9781501738548 (pbk. ; alk. paper)
Subjects: LCSH: Election districts—United States—Maps. | United States.
    Congress—Election districts—Maps. | Digital mapping—United States.
Classification: LCC JK1341 (ebook) | LCC JK1341 .A54 2018 (print) |
    DDC 328.73/07345—dc23
LC record available at https://lccn.loc.gov/2018038389

Contents

Contents

Acknowledgments

The Public Mapping Project builds upon the conviction that an engaged public can create better governance by being active participants in public policy making. Our focus is *redistricting*, the periodic redrawing of district boundaries to achieve better representation—or at least that's the idea. Seemingly arcane requirements demand analyses of large amounts of data manipulated by tricky software applications. A steep technological learning curve serves politicians' interests, since it shuts the public out of the process, allowing those in power to draw districts that meet their goals, with little public oversight. We wish to lower these technological barriers and foster greater public participation and transparency whenever states and cities draw their legislative boundaries.

Many people share our vision and helped make it a reality. Public mapping cannot exist without the public, so foremost, we would like to thank the hundreds, if not thousands, of people who have drawn their own maps using our District Builder software or similar applications. Their creativity helped reveal how to build better districts. We are also grateful to the many teachers and professors who brought public mapping into their classrooms and volunteered their time to help their students learn and participate in this vital democratic process.

We could not have done our work without generous support from donors. Larry Hansen at the Joyce Foundation was an early supporter of redistricting reform action, and we remember him with deep fondness. Daniel Goroff at the Sloan Foundation has been instrumental in providing support for DistrictBuilder's development. Other organizations that have contributed support include the William Penn Foundation, the Judy Ford Wason Center for Public Policy at Christopher Newport University, and Amazon Corporation. Robert Cheetham and the crew at Azavea Corporation took the lead in developing our software. It would not exist without their extensive—and sometimes even pro bono—efforts.

Much of our work in educating the public on redistricting arose from a collaboration with the Brennan Center for Justice at New York University. Justin Levitt, now at Loyola Law School, authored the *A Citizen's Guide to Redistricting* and maintains the All About Redistricting website. Other Brennan Center collaborators include Kesha Gaskins, Michael Li, Myna Perez, and Wendy Weiser.

Thomas Mann arranged for us to become Visiting Fellows at the Brookings Institution, and he and Norm Ornstein at the American Enterprise Institute served as co-chairs of our advisory board. Other advisory board members who graciously donated their time include Mike Fortner, Republican Illinois State Representative (95th District); Carling Dinker, staff member to Democratic U.S. Representative John Tanner (TN-8); Mary Wilson, past president of the League of Women Voters; Derek Cressman, then the western regional director of state operations, Common Cause; Gerry Hebert, executive director and director of litigation of the Campaign Legal Center; Nancy Bekavac, director of Scientists and Engineers for America; Leah Rush, executive director of the Midwest Democracy Network; Anthony Fairfax, president of Census Channel; Karin Mac Donald, director of the California Statewide Database at the Institute for Government Studies, University of California, Berkeley; and Kim Brace, president of Elections Data Services.

Leah Rush deserves special mention. She helped us coordinate with Midwest Democracy Network's members as we promoted public mapping education and opportunities in Illinois, Indiana, Michigan, Minnesota, Ohio, and Wisconsin. We wish we could name all the members of the MDN who assisted us in this effort, and we would especially like to thank Catherine Turcer with Ohio Common Cause; Cynthia Canary with Illinois Campaign for Political Reform; Mike

Dean with Minnesota Common Cause; and Jocelyn Bensen at Wayne State University. We had help in other states, too. Quentin Kidd at Christopher Newport University helped us launch the first Virginia redistricting competition. Costas Panagopoulos hosted a New York student competition while he was at Fordham University. Mark Salling at Cleveland State University assisted us with Ohio's redistricting database. Our Mexico collaborators Alejandro Trelles at Brandeis University and Eric Magar at Instituto Tecnológico Autónomo de México arranged productive exchanges with the Mexican government and helped us launch DistrictBuilder there.

Michael McDonald served as lead author, authored early versions of the manuscript and was responsible for redrafting the manuscript in its current form; Micah Altman and Michael McDonald co-led in the conception of the work, including the core ideas, analytical framework, and statement of research questions. All authors contributed to research and analysis and to the writing process through direct writing, critical review, and commentary.

Our mentors cultivated our interest in redistricting. Gary King brought us together by hiring us as his research associates at Harvard University. We are deeply indebted to other scholars: Bruce Cain at Stanford University; Gary Cox at Stanford University; Bernard Grofman at University of California, Irvine; Morgan Kousser at California Institute of Technology; David Lublin at American University, Arthur Lupia at the University of Michigan; Daniel Smith at the

University of Florida; Kenneth McCue at California Institute of Technology; and Brian Amos, a recent University of Florida PhD graduate. We've had productive relationships with a number of others, too, including Jeff Reichart, producer of the documentary *Gerrymandering*; Peter Wattson, former general counsel for the Minnesota Senate; John Guthrie, staff director at the Committee on Reapportionment Florida Senate; Jim Wisely, a California political consultant; Wendy Underhill and Tim Storey at the National Conference of State Legislatures; Douglas Johnson at National Demographics Corporation; and Tom Bonior at TargetSmart.

We extend our gratitude to everyone who has been part of this journey.

THE PUBLIC
MAPPING
PROJECT

1

Introduction

In 2013, Minneapolis voters elected Abdi Warsame and Alondra Cano to their city council. Both were historic candidates. Warsame defeated an incumbent to become the first Somali to be elected to the city council; indeed, at the time, he became the highest elected official of Somali descent in the United States. And as the first Mexican American elected to that office, Cano's election was a breakthrough, too. These remarkable individuals were aided, in part, by an arcane process known as redistricting, which fashioned voting districts that offered Somali and Mexican-American communities the opportunity to elect a candidate of their choice. The manner by which these districts were drawn— by the public directly, meeting a complex set of conditions— serves as a blueprint for how the public can be engaged in redistricting to serve the representational needs of communities, rather than the self-serving interests of politicians.

We describe our efforts to empower the public. Too often, politicians draw districts out of the public's sight to accomplish their political ends. These districts assist the reelection of incumbents, deny representation to persons of color, and help one party win a legislative majority even when most voters choose candidates from the other party. Our public mapping efforts across the country reveal a fundamentally different approach to redistricting: one that allows the public to draw its own fully legal districts that are politically fair, protect and even enhance minority representation, and respect local community boundaries. These wildly divergent results flag the urgent need for transparency and public participation in redistricting.

Our perspectives on public mapping are informed by nearly three decades of being active participants in state and local redistricting efforts and litigation across the United States. We have analyzed data and developed software for our scholarly pursuits and advocacy work. During a 2010 round of redistricting, we created open-source, web-accessible redistricting software called DistrictBuilder in collaboration with Azavea, a Philadelphia GIS company. We deployed it in states and localities across the United States to enable ordinary people to draw legally admissible redistricting plans. This book is a reflection on our experiences from a practical and (dare we say) academic viewpoint. We learned a lot beyond simply doing software project management. We helped build grassroots coalitions for public mapping, educated the public and policymakers about the need for transparency and public participation, and did the things academics tend to do, such as building and analyzing datasets. This book is an extension of our work to educate, encourage, and empower.

History and Background

Everywhere in the United States, candidates are elected by the districts they are campaigning to represent: it's true for local offices like city council and school boards, state legislatures, and the national Congress. Districts serve an important purpose, which is to identify the community that an elected government official must represent. Every decade, new district lines are drawn to equalize districts' populations to ensure that some people do not receive more representation than others.

In theory, governments do this work to achieve relatively neutral administrative goals such as drawing nicely shaped districts that follow existing political or geographic boundaries, and to allow communities with shared interests an opportunity to be represented together. In practice, the people in charge of drawing districts for political offices are state legislators, and they have a vested interest in how these districts are drawn. Once elected, politicians manipulate boundaries by slicing and dicing communities to assist their personal reelection, win legislative majorities for their political party, and deny representation to communities of color. You may be familiar with this malpractice as *gerrymandering*, which was coined in 1812 to mock a salamander-shaped Massachusetts state senate district signed into law by Governor Elbridge Gerry. The original gerrymander was so effective that the Federalists—Governor Gerry's political opponents—won only 27 percent of the seats in the next election despite winning a narrow majority of the vote. The gerrymander lives on. Most recently, these alarming anti-majoritarian outcomes occurred during the 1996 and 2012 congressional elections, and during recent Michigan, Pennsylvania, Virginia, and Wisconsin state legislative elections.

An important redistricting element is population data. Every ten years since the founding of the republic, the federal government has conducted a census that determines the number of seats each state will have for the following decade. For a long time, a change in the number of congressional representatives did not necessarily trigger the drawing of new district boundaries, because some states elected their members in at-large statewide districts instead; congressional, state, and local districts were not required to be representative of a given state's population. But in the 1960s, the Supreme Court found districts of unequal populations, a practice known as *malapportionment*, to violate the US Constitution, thus setting in motion the decennial ritual of redistricting following a new national census. Later that decade, the federal government passed into law the Voting Rights

Act, which effectively prohibited the worst racial gerrymandering practices. Still, states and localities have wide latitude within federal limits to draw districts to protect incumbents and help political parties.

Reform advocates are pursuing two pathways to reduce political self-dealing during redistricting. An approach that would strike a blow to partisan gerrymandering throughout the United States is to have the Supreme Court adopt an anti-partisan gerrymandering judicial standard, much as it did to outlaw malapportionment. Another approach is for reformers to engage state-by-state by bringing lawsuits to enforce existing state regulations, amending state constitutions, or passing new laws to create new regulations.

There remains a hope that the US Supreme Court could outlaw partisan gerrymandering. The nine-member court is divided with four liberal justices who believe partisan gerrymandering is unconstitutional and that a standard exists to identify when violations occur. Two conservative justices do not believe partisan gerrymandering is unconstitutional. As of this writing, two conservative justices rejected statewide partisan gerrymandering claims but appear willing to entertain single-district challenges. A ninth member's position is unknown, and Justice Kennedy's retirement creates substantial uncertainty in this area.

Reform advocates have had more success with state supreme courts, which struck down redistricting plans in Florida and Pennsylvania for being excessive partisan gerrymanders in violation of their state constitutions.

Pennsylvania's court interpreted a long-standing clause requiring elections to be "free and equal" to prohibit partisan gerrymandering. Florida's court looked to a voter-approved 2010 amendment to the constitution that states, "No apportionment plan or individual district shall be drawn with the intent to favor or disfavor a political party or an incumbent." In both of these states, the legislature still has a direct role in drawing districts, and it is up to the courts to enforce their constitutions. Seven other states have similar prohibitions, but there has been no favorable court action to enforce them.

In other states, reformers have changed the redistricting process by placing it in the hands of a commission that works independent of the legislature. Reformers generally regard the Arizona and California commissions as their reform model. These commissions have four desirable characteristics:

1. Vetting: a state agency vets prospective members to root out people with obvious conflicts of interest.

2. Clear districting guidelines: while drawing districts, the commission must abide by a set of well-defined criteria.[1]

3. Transparency: the commission must operate in the open.

4. Public comments: the commission must solicit and accept public input into how districts should be drawn.

Because politicians are loath to give up their power voluntarily, redistricting reforms usually occur through a ballot initiative that empowers voters to have their say. Reform through a ballot initiative is difficult, however, and only available in about half of the states that permit it.[2] Petition circulators must first collect signatures from registered voters who want the question to appear on the ballot. If enough valid signatures are collected, a statewide campaign—typically costing millions of dollars—must educate the public about the issue. If the party in control of state government opposes reform, the ballot initiative will often fail; their supporters take the cue from their leaders to vote against it. If fortune favors the reformers, however, the initiative may be adopted.

The good news for reformers is that the public is generally on their side. Advocacy groups have successfully reformed state redistricting processes through voter approval of ballot questions in Arizona, California, Florida, Ohio, and Washington. At the time of this printing, active advocacy efforts are underway in more states. Not all reform efforts have been successful. Prior efforts failed in California, Florida, and Ohio, and South Dakota voters recently rejected a reform proposal. Still, the successes outnumber the failures, and reformers can learn from their mistakes to successfully try again.

Public Mapping: Our Model for Success

One of these reform efforts occurred in the city of Minneapolis, where reformers wished to demonstrate the viability of reform by starting local. The Minneapolis city council districts were formerly drawn by a bipartisan commission appointed directly by the city council, setting up the possibility of political self-dealing through gerry-mandering. In 2010, Minneapolis voters approved a Charter Amendment that transferred redistricting power to the city's Charter Commission, which is appointed by the chief judge of the Hennepin County District Court.[3] (Minneso-tans tend to trust judges with governance, a reform model that is not shared widely elsewhere.) The Charter Commission, in turn, solicited interested members of the public to serve on the nine-member Redistricting Group to advise the commission on the drawing of new city council districts. The Charter Commission established criteria to guide the Redistricting Group, notably keeping communities of interest in a single city council ward, where possible. For those who could not serve on the Redistricting Group but still wanted to be involved in the deliberations, the Charter Commission invited suggestions from the public.

Working with a state-based advocacy group, Draw the Line Minnesota, we put our DistrictBuilder software into the hands of interested members of the public, empowering them to provide their suggestions to Minneapolis' Redistricting Group during the public comment period. As mentioned, DistrictBuilder allows mapping novices to draw legal districts through their web browsers, without having to be experts in geographic information software. (We discuss

DistrictBuilder in greater detail in the following chapters.) Redistricting Group members had purchased a single desktop version of a commercial redistricting software to accomplish their task, which they found inconvenient to use, so members began using DistrictBuilder from their offices and homes. So, too, did two community-based groups: a Latino community group and the Citizens Committee for Fair Redistricting led by Abdi Warsame. In all, users generated thirty-eight city council maps using our software.

Citizens Committee for Fair Redistricting advocated for the creation of a predominantly East African Ward 6. The Latino group advocated for increasing the Hispanic population of Ward 9. Through DistrictBuilder's sharing features, these groups were able to share their ideas with the Minneapolis Redistricting Group, which incorporated the draft district maps into their working plan. The result of this collaboration between the public and the Redistricting Group resulted in changes to the city council ward districts.

Figure 1.1 shows the African American community located around Ward 6 prior to the redistricting. The census blocks are shaded by the proportion of the population that is African American. Most of the nonshaded census blocks are composed primarily of businesses or other zero-population blocks that are difficult to display in a monochromatic color scheme. The community was spread across four districts: Ward 2, Ward 6, Ward 7, and Ward 8. Following the redistricting, the African American community was consolidated

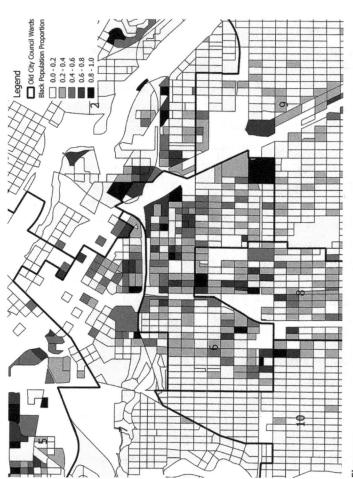

Figure 1.1

within Ward 6, as shown in figure 1.2. As a result, Ward 6's non-Hispanic black population was increased from 26 percent to 45 percent. Figure 1.3 shows the Hispanic community located around Ward 9 before the redistricting. The community was effectively divided among three districts, Wards 6, 8, and 9. Following the redistricting, the community was consolidated into Ward 9, as shown in figure 1.4. Ward 9's Hispanic population was increased from 17 percent to 37 percent. And you already know what happened in the new districts after the election: the first Somali American and Mexican American gained seats on the Minneapolis city council, giving voice to communities that previously were unrepresented there.

These maps help illustrate why redistricting is so important to representation. An effective gerrymandering strategy denies representation to communities of color and other politically cohesive communities. Here, African American and Hispanic communities were spread across several districts, a gerrymandering strategy known as *cracking*. Cracking dilutes the voting power of a community such that they cannot elect a candidate of their choice among any of the districts they are cracked among. Another effective gerrymandering strategy is known as *packing*, whereby a community's voters are concentrated within a single district, thereby by wasting their votes in a district their candidate of choice wins by an overwhelming margin. A happy medium between these two extremes affords the best representation, where a

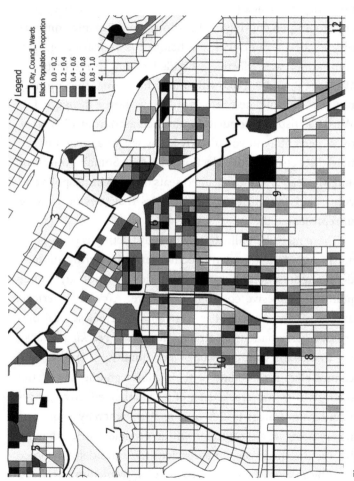

Figure 1.2

Figure 1.3

Figure 1.4

community is neither cracked or packed so that they can have an effective say in their representation.

We have supported public mapping efforts like Minneapolis's in states and localities across the United States, and even in Mexico. Minneapolis was our greatest success in demonstrating that by giving the public the data and tools, they can be full partners in the redistricting process. We had other successes and failures. In this essay, we reflect upon our experiences with public mapping, how it beats the current process to create better outcomes, how to do your own public mapping, and how your efforts can be an important part of the redistricting reform agenda.

2

A History of Public Mapping

Public mapping is intimately intertwined with evolving legal standards and technological innovation. The public has drawn redistricting plans for at least half a century, when the Washington State League of Women Voters first proposed redistricting plans in support of their reform efforts in the 1950s. The earliest efforts were made possible because districts were primarily drawn out of large geographic units such as counties, which greatly simplified the redistricting task. That task grew more complex in the early 1960s, when the Supreme Court ruled that districts had to be of roughly equal population: counties would now often have to be split between two or more districts.

The equal population requirement became more exacting as the Census Bureau released more population statistics for smaller geographic units. These increasing computational demands effectively shut the public out of redistricting, since redistricting could be performed only on extremely costly computer systems. The reemergence of public mapping began in the 1990s, when states began offering public access to computer terminals loaded with their redistricting software and data. In the 2000s, lower hardware costs and the emergence of commercial software vendors continued to make redistricting systems more accessible, but they were still within reach of only well-funded public interest organizations that had mappers with technical skills.

Two technological innovations by 2010 made public mapping available to the general public. Organizations and individuals willing to provide the public goods of software development and data dissemination are now able to leverage high-speed internet and open-source software to disseminate easy-to-use redistricting systems through the web, making redistricting accessible to anyone from high school students to retirees.

Early Public Mapping

The redistricting task was much simpler before the landmark 1960s US Supreme Court decisions that mandated districts must be of equal population.[4] Prior to 1962, *redistricting* was often synonymous with *apportionment*, which is a formula that assigns legislative seats to localities (e.g., counties and townships) based on their population. In their purest forms, apportionment formulas worked by assigning at least one legislative seat to each locality, with larger localities perhaps receiving more. A locality that was apportioned more than one seat did not necessarily trigger redistricting, as two or more legislators might be selected by at-large elections run across the entire locality. Not all states worked in this manner. Some state constitutions required districts of (somewhat) equal populations, which meant grouping rural localities into districts and drawing more than one district within the more populous localities.

For states that employed redistricting in this era, the task was such that one could draw a legal plan by making a map of counties while referring to a table of population statistics. This could still be a surprisingly costly, labor-intensive enterprise. One report priced New York's early 1960s redistricting effort at $100,000, which is about $750,000 when adjusted for inflation.[5] Therefore, only organizations with substantial interests and resources could produce legal districts, which is why redistricting work primarily fell to governments and political parties. The earliest example we can identify of extra-governmental public mapping occurred in 1954, when the Washington State League of Women Voters created a state legislative plan with input from their local chapters as a demonstration of reform possibilities.[6] This effort eventually led to the adoption of one of the first redistricting commissions in the country.[7]

Some states avoided redistricting altogether by simply refusing to draw new districts, leading to gross population imbalances as urban populations grew faster relative to rural areas. This situation, known as malapportionment, meant less-populous, rural areas effectively had more representation than faster-growing urban areas. Perhaps the worst offender was Connecticut, whose state legislature's lower chamber had two representatives from the state capital of Hartford, with a population over 177,000 persons, and two from the town of Union, with 261 persons.[8] In the 1960s, the US Supreme Court, which had been reluctant to enter the political thicket of redistricting in deference to the political process, ordered that districts at all levels of government must be of roughly equal population.

Redistricting is like a jigsaw puzzle: the more pieces, the more difficult the puzzle. The Supreme Court's rulings added complications that meant some less-populous localities would have to be combined into a single district and larger counties and towns would have to be broken up into smaller geographic units so that all districts contained about the same number of people. At the time, governments typically drew their districts out of the Census Bureau geographic unit known as a census tract, which contains roughly a few thousand people. Still, the scale of the problem was not as large as modern standards. Back then, a state might have hundreds of census tracts. Presently, districts are drawn out of even smaller geographic units known as census blocks. In urban areas, census blocks are often the size of a typical street block, but they follow just about every physical feature that delineates a boundary—streams, road medians, and more. There are hundreds of census blocks in a tract, and there are also more tracts, increasing the scale of the redistricting task by orders of magnitude.

In the early 1960s, James Weaver and Sidney Hess, two Delaware operations research engineers who collaborated with a Delaware good-government group known as the Committee of 39, developed one of the first computer redistricting programs.[9] The automated algorithm was far from easy to use, as the census tract data and their program were encoded onto punch cards that were fed through a mainframe computer. These advocates ran their program to create districts for Delaware's local and state legislative bodies, and then drew additional maps by hand. Although governments and courts considered their plans, none was formally adopted for use. While these individuals failed to achieve their advocacy goals, their technical innovations blazed the path for the development of more sophisticated computer software to assist in sifting through the mountains of geographic and demographic redistricting data.

While the equal population rulings of the 1960s forced redistricting across the country to rectify malapportionment, the availability of census tract data meant that there was some leeway in how equal districts' populations had to be. In the 1970s, the Census Bureau began releasing more population data for a greater number of census blocks.[10] As this more detailed information became available, the courts continued to impose more exacting equal population requirements. Today, practitioners and legal scholars widely believe that congressional districts should deviate by no more than one person, to prevent a potential equal population legal challenge. State legislative and local districts can deviate by no more than 10 percent between the most and least populated district.[11] In addition, the Voting Rights Act requires the creation of districts to elect minority candidates of choice by meeting acceptable levels of minority population within districts. Governments often find a need to draw districts out of census blocks to comply with the Voting Rights Act; larger geographic boundaries such as census tracts don't follow community boundaries well.

As redistricting data demands increased, well-funded state governments turned to computers to assist in the data tabulation to ensure compliance with equal population mandates.[12] In the 1970s, Iowa, Delaware, and Washington developed tabulation systems. Illinois, Michigan, and New York followed in the 1980s. California also created a system in the 1980s, but did not deploy it until after new districts were adopted. The price tag for the data compilation, hardware, and software systems ran into the hundreds of thousands and even millions of dollars. Today, we take for granted how accessible computers are: they are in our phones, appliances, cars, and many other facets of daily life. Like the Delaware experiment, a typical redistricting system ran on a mainframe computer housed in a clean room, and early systems used punch cards or electronic tapes for data entry and programming. These technology requirements effectively shut the public out of the redistricting process. Even in states where computers were not used, these data demands increased so much that only the best-funded organizations—governments or political parties, as mentioned earlier—could afford the labor costs involved to draw districts manually.[13]

The Rebirth of Public Mapping

If computer-enabled complexity effectively killed public participation in redistricting, continued technological innovations would lower costs such that the public could reengage. Innovations in data storage allowed the Census Bureau and governments to distribute the large volume of redistricting data in more accessible media. The rise of workstations and personal computers meant clean rooms and mainframe computers were no longer necessary to process these data. Companies distributed general commercial geographic information systems (GIS) software at a lower cost, and some states even distributed homegrown redistricting systems cheaply or free. An important innovation was the development of graphical user interfaces on a computer terminal, which visualized the task at hand. This innovation hid the underlying programming from users so that they could concentrate on assigning geography to districts.

Despite these innovations, still only well-funded organizations could afford a redistricting system. Furthermore, only skilled users could coerce general GIS applications into producing the summary reports needed to evaluate whether a redistricting plan met legal requirements. A 1991 National Conference of State Legislatures' survey of redistricting practices found the average system cost half a million dollars.[14] What precipitated the rebirth of public mapping was that fifteen states reported providing a computer terminal loaded with a redistricting system for public use. Access to these terminals was limited, however. Adventurous mappers needed to be able to travel to the location of the terminal, perhaps in a state capital or state library, and compete with others for screen time. Twenty-two state governments disseminated redistricting data—census data that was sometimes augmented with election data—for outside organizations that wished to attempt drawing districts. If the public could successfully create a redistricting plan, twenty-four states would consider these public submissions. Despite these advancements, only well-organized public interest groups are known to have submitted plans, such as the National Association of the Advancement for Colored People and the Mexican-American Legal Defense and Education Fund.[15]

By 2000, more state and local governments demanded redistricting software, which expanded the market and allowed commercial GIS vendors such as Caliper Corporation and Digital Engineering Corporation to develop specialized redistricting systems that could run on a high-end personal computer. These offerings were markedly cheaper than their predecessors, but the licensing costs were still outside a common person's budget, running about the same as a low-end new car. Florida, Hawaii, Ohio, and Wisconsin developed homegrown applications that individuals could theoretically run on their computers. (We say "theoretically" because we attempted unsuccessfully to install one state's redistricting system on our computers.)

A Florida application known as FREDS for Florida REDistricting Software, was innovative in that it was a specialized desktop system usable with minimal training. It came preloaded with data, and the commands were limited to redistricting tasks rather than being a generalized GIS program with a redistricting add-on. These advances would be generally embraced in the next decade, by ourselves and others. FREDS sold for $20, but to our knowledge was never used in another state's redistricting because only Florida government employees had access to the source code to modify the software for out-of-state use.

Another innovation of the 2000s was the growing maturity of the internet. Thirty-four states created redistricting websites. States disseminated redistricting data through twenty-four of these sites, two disseminated data by other means, and the US Census Bureau disseminated geographic boundaries and population data for all states through their website. Thirty-four states accepted public submissions and other feedback, most often through their web portals. While the general movement was toward greater access to data and software, there was minor retrenchment, with one state citing their website as a reason for discontinuing sponsorship of their public terminal.

We don't know the full scope of public participation in the 2000 round of redistricting. However, among the better documented examples is Arizona's Independent Redistricting Commission (AIRC). The AIRC was adopted through a 2000 ballot initiative and embodies characteristics of what many advocates consider the best reform model.[16] This commission reform model has four components mentioned in chapter 1: vetting of prospective commissioners, well-defined criteria, a window for public input and feedback, and public meetings. At the time, these requirements fostered the greatest transparency and openness to public input of any state redistricting authority in the history of the United States.

A record of the AIRC's work during redistricting efforts in the 2000s is available online.[17] The AIRC held numerous public hearings across the state to solicit public input. The Arizona constitution requires the commission to respect communities of interest, and many individuals, organizations, and local governments expressed their community boundaries to the commission in verbal comments. In addition, outside organizations and individuals presented proposed districts and complete redistricting plans to the commission. The Democratic Party presented congressional and state legislative plans.[18] So did the Navajo Nation and the Eastern Arizona Counties Association.[19] Arizona Democratic congressman Ed Pastor submitted partial congressional and state legislative plans, as well, with the intent to meet legal voting rights obligations to provide opportunities for minority communities of choice. Another coalition of local elected officials and local activists, known as the Minority Coalition for Fair Redistricting, supported these districts, with some proposed modifications.[20] Yet if the Arizona commission was the most ambitious for public participation at the time, its public mapping was still limited to well-funded organizations like political parties or minority advocacy groups.

Modern Public Mapping

At last, the general public has gained access to the same data and software as political parties and well-organized interests thanks to three technological innovations realized by the 2010 round of redistricting. The first is the increasing speed of the internet, which makes online mapping applications possible. The latest generation of redistricting software can perform its computationally intensive calculations on a server that users access through their web browsers, meaning that these users no longer need to purchase and install software on their home devices. A fast internet is desirable, since redistricting applications push a lot of data through the internet between servers and browsers.

A second innovation is the development of the cloud computing infrastructure. A mapper who wishes to create legal districts for most places must draw districts out of the small and numerous census blocks. While computing power has continued to increase, a high-end machine with lots of memory and hefty processors is still needed to process these complex demands. Fortunately, users no longer need to invest in this kind of complete, high-end system—instead, they can buy access to extensible servers on the Amazon or Google cloud computing infrastructure. An account holder can increase the server capacity when demand is high, scale it back when demand is low, and turn it off when not in use.

A third innovation is the maturity of open-source software that enables developers to create complex mapping applications at a lower software development cost. Among these new open-source, web-based applications is District-Builder, which we developed and deployed in collaboration with the GIS software firm Azavea. We are not the only game in town. Another popular free application is David Bradlee's self-named Dave's Redistricting App, which is installed on home computers.[21] Both chambers of the Florida legislature independently created and deployed online redistricting apps, too. And, of course, there are commercial players such as ERSI's Maptitude and CityGate's Autobound.[22]

These developments have made true public mapping possible through the development of redistricting software designed for use by novices. Much like Florida's FREDS application used a decade ago, an administrator simply configures the software with the necessary geographic, population, and election data and sets up metrics to meet legal requirements. This newest mapping applications, however, are easily configurable and deployable across all fifty states and around the world. Public mapping can now happen everywhere.

3

Planning for Public Mapping

We supported public mapping efforts in states and localities across the United States and even in Mexico. We call our work the *Public Mapping Project*, and its guiding principles are to increase transparency and participation in the redistricting process by providing the public with the tools and data needed to draw and evaluate redistricting plans. We don't expect every person to draw maps. Indeed, only a little more than half the eligible electorate votes in a presidential election. What we hope is that having enough eyes on the problem will give policymakers a better sense of their available options, and permit objective observers—the public, media, and courts—to determine whether there are better ways to achieve redistricting goals.

We call our effort the *Public* Mapping Project rather than the *Citizen* Mapping Project for a specific reason that is important for those considering similar activities. The voting rights community, particularly Latino and Asian organizations, are sensitive to using words like *citizen* to describe advocacy efforts affecting communities that have substantial numbers of legal, noncitizen immigrants. As a matter of inclusive messaging we listened to these communities and decided to use the word *public* to signify our efforts.

The project's success is the culmination of four activities. First, we educated the public on redistricting, with an aim to generate buy-in among grassroots advocacy groups to our idea of public mapping. Second, we developed the District-Builder software to provide redistricting tools to the public (more on this in chapter 4). Third, we compiled census and election data to include with the software. Fourth, we worked with state-based partners to support public mapping efforts in their states. We learned a lot through our notable successes and failures. The purpose of this chapter is to provide a how-to guide for conducting public mapping advocacy, using our perspective on what has and has not worked for us in the past.

Public Education and Building Coalitions

The significant interest in redistricting reform today has its roots in the patronage of Larry Hansen, a vice president of the Joyce Foundation, which is a Chicago charitable foundation active in the Midwestern states.[23] Following the turn of the millennium, Larry created the Midwest Democracy Network, an interstate association of grassroots government reform organizations. Larry was a leader in the sphere of charitable foundations, having successfully raised public awareness for campaign finance reform, culminating in the 2002 Bipartisan Campaign Finance Reform Act. The Midwest Democracy Network would serve as a vehicle for generating advocacy around redistricting and other reform issues.

Following the campaign finance reform model, Larry's first step was to create educational materials for public consumption. He reached out to Michael McDonald, who was developing a reputation in redistricting through his scholarship, his practical work as a consultant for redistricting authorities, and as an expert witness in redistricting lawsuits. Larry funded a collaboration between Michael and Justin Levitt, then at the Brennan Center, which resulted in the creation of *A Citizen's Guide to Redistricting*, a primer to explain the arcane redistricting process to a layperson. (Its name sparked the discussion about the advantages of the word *public* over *citizen*.) This book is available online at no cost.[24] Justin and Michael toured the Midwestern states to educate the public on redistricting, with Midwest Democracy Network partners hosting public forums in advance of the 2010 round of redistricting.

The involvement of state-based advocacy groups is an important ingredient in a successful public education forum.

These groups have often been involved in their states' government reform efforts for decades. They know the best locations to hold a forum. They know the major players in state government who might participate, adding gravitas to an event. They know the reporters who work the state government beats, who will be interested in covering a well-organized event. They are instrumental, in some cases, in arranging for the forum to be broadcast on the state's public television stations. Most important, they can reach out through their networks to attract an audience.

These forums were meant to educate the public on redistricting, but they also helped develop buy-in among these groups for reform efforts. After we held the public forums, partners of the Midwest Democracy Network developed strategies for their redistricting advocacy. The Joyce Foundation provided tools to assist them, such as funding polls and retaining a public relations company to assist with media plans, but each state-based group decided what form their advocacy would take. All of these state-based organizations adopted some form of public mapping. Sadly, Larry Hansen would not live to see the fruits of his efforts, as he passed away in 2010, before redistricting began.

Our Past Efforts

We supported redistricting efforts in states other than in the Midwest. In Virginia we worked with a coalition of Republican-leaning business leaders who supported Governor Robert McDonnell's political campaign in part because he pledged to support redistricting reform. When he reneged on his promise, these individuals approached Michael for advocacy ideas. At the time, Michael was a professor at George Mason University, located in Northern Virginia, and had been speaking at events across the state on redistricting issues. These funders provided support through the Judy Ford Wason Center for Public Policy at Christopher Newport University for a student redistricting competition. (Judy Ford Wason was one of these influential leaders.) Later, to preempt the student competition, Gov. McDonnell issued an executive order creating an Independent Bipartisan Advisory Redistricting Commission. The competition's technical infrastructure and map ideas generated by the student participants were rolled into the governor's commission.

Similarly, Azavea has been instrumental in supporting advocacy efforts in their home state of Pennsylvania. They assisted with the Fix Philly competition to draw Philadelphia city council districts. In the wake of important Pennsylvania Supreme Court ruling curtailing partisan gerrymandering for the state's legislative and congressional districts, Azavea is working with the Committee of Seventy, a Pennsylvania-based reform group, to host a redistricting competition to advocate for institutional reform of the state's redistricting process.

While we've had successes, we've had failures, too. Our Arizona experience is a cautionary tale of what happens when grassroots advocacy capacity is lacking. In 2011, we were approached by former Arizona state representative Ken Clark, who led the Arizona Competitive Districts Coalition, to support public mapping in his state. We were eager to work with the coalition because the Arizona Independent Redistricting Commission is tasked with promoting, and being responsive to, public input. We prepared the necessary data and Azavea assisted the Arizona Competitive Districts Coalition to deploy DistrictBuilder.[25] The group held a redistricting competition,[26] and on October 13, 2011, it submitted three winning maps for the commission's consideration.[27] Despite this activity, the coalition appears to be a transient group that did not have a tangible effect on Arizona's redistricting process. The coalition's website is now defunct and their Facebook page dormant. Ken Clark spoke at some of the early AIRC meetings, but did not appear at later meetings. His absence was most noticeable at the meetings held concurrent to the submission of the winning maps to the AIRC, and commission did not acknowledge the coalition's map submissions at their public hearings. Ultimately, the budget fell short of the effort we invested.

Our New York experience is another sort of cautionary tale: what happens when we act as interlopers promoting an agenda that may be in competition with state-based advocacy groups. The Sloan Foundation, which supported the

DistrictBuilder software development, is located in New York City and has a special mission focused on improving the lives of New Yorkers. They wanted to deploy District-Builder to support a New York redistricting competition, but unlike our past efforts in other states, we did not have a state-based partner.

There are two major New York advocacy groups that advocate for redistricting reform: Citizens Union and Common Cause of New York. Citizens Union concentrated their efforts on reforming the redistricting process and did not believe drawing alternative maps were compatible with their reform strategy. Common Cause is a national federation of state-based groups, so while we worked closely with Common Cause organizations in the Midwest, we had little communication with the New York chapter. Common Cause of New York was interested in public mapping, and we offered to support them at no cost to them because we had Sloan funding; however, they decided to partner with *Newsday*, a Long Island newspaper, and use Dave's Redistricting App. Lacking cooperation from state-based groups, we partnered with Costas Panagopoulous, at the time a Fordham University political science professor, to hold a university student competition.

In some respects, our efforts were a success. Students from across New York participated in the competition. When the congressional redistricting ended in state government gridlock, the court-appointed special master, Nate Persily, appears to have considered some of the student ideas, particularly around the Buffalo area. (A Common Cause plan had similar features, so we cannot know if this was an example of evolutionary convergence.) However, to our surprise, Common Cause of New York and *Newsday* threatened to sue us for downloading a plan posted on their website and loading it into DistrictBuilder, claiming that their public policy proposal was copyrighted. Following tense phone calls and email exchanges, we decided that while we had a strong case to display their plan under the "fair use" legal doctrine, we would delete the offending plan from our software because we did not want to divert attention from our mutual reform goals by taking our disagreement public.

The experiences of Pennsylvania and Virginia demonstrate that having a well-organized interstate group like the Midwest Democracy Network is helpful, but not necessary, in building a successful coalition for public mapping. However, advocacy efforts do not materialize out of thin air. Our Arizona experience demonstrates there must be in-state capacity to execute reform advocacy, and our New York experience underscores the need to bring together potential coalition partners. The fault lies on us, because in our eagerness, we overextended our efforts into states that we suspected would be challenging. The Funders Committee for Civic Participation has expanded Larry's vision for the Midwest Democracy Network to provide a backbone for redistricting advocacy across the country, which should help build capacity and in-state coordination for reform efforts, including public mapping.

Redistricting Competitions

A popular form of public mapping advocacy is redistricting competitions. Running up to the 2010 round of redistricting, Ohio reformers partnered with the Ohio secretary of state Jennifer Brunner to hold the first redistricting competition, to our knowledge.[28] The competition was intended primarily to capture the public's imagination for reform—it used stale 2000 census data, and no active redistricting was taking place yet in Ohio. We built upon Ohio's experience in 2011 when Virginia reformers executed the first redistricting competition while a state government was in the midst of the redistricting process. We subsequently supported competitions in Arizona, Michigan, Minnesota, New York, Ohio, Pennsylvania, and the City of Philadelphia. We are also aware of a Tennessee competition using Dave's Redistricting App.

Planning

There are a number of elements to a successful redistricting competition, aside from having an in-state organization with the capacity to carry it out. At the outset, a group needs to create a strategic plan for their competition. Having a plan helps execute a competition, of course, but it is also necessary to raise money; potential funders want to know how their money will be spent. A group needs ample lead time to create and execute their plan. If a competition is to happen while redistricting is taking place, we recommend developing a strategic plan no later than the beginning of the year of the decennial census. This should provide enough lead time to run the competition the following year, when the all-important census population data are released, which triggers redistricting.

Tools

There are software and data costs that are sufficiently technical in nature that we mention them in passing now, and expand upon them in the next chapter. Commercial online redistricting applications are available, but are likely too expensive for an advocacy group. Dave's Redistricting App is free, although not open-source, and it is great for what it does—create example plans using pre-supplied data; but as of this writing, it cannot draw legal redistricting plans in most cases due to shortcuts the application takes to make it performant, nor does it enable configuration with other data or contests, nor produce statistics to gauge how well a plan meets all legal requirements. A redistricting commission or legislature thus may not seriously consider plans created with this software. Still, Dave's Redistricting App may be sufficient to demonstrate the existence of alternative possibilities.

DistrictBuilder sits halfway between these applications. The software is free, open-source, can draw legal redistricting plans, is broadly configurable, and produces statistics to help guide users. But if you plan a hefty installation, one that can support many simultaneous users—as occurs with a redistricting competition—it incurs setup and server costs that can run about ten to twenty thousand dollars. As of this writing, we are working to lower these costs through automated data provisioning and deployment on the cloud computing infrastructure.

Parameters and Judging

A redistricting competition organizer needs to consider what participants will attempt to achieve. Will participants draw redistricting plans to meet legal criteria or to embody aspirational advocacy goals? In the former case, there are a number of online resources that describe federal and state requirements, such as Justin Levitt's "All About Redistricting," the Brennan Center's "50 State Guide," and the National Conference of State Legislature's redistricting page.[29] These resources are valuable but can be incomplete, particularly when state legislative committees responsible for drafting maps adopt additional guidelines. An organization should monitor such legislative committees closely.

In the latter case, the competition hosts need to agree on their goals, such as grading maps on partisan fairness and the number of competitive districts, goals that are formally required in few states. Of course, there can be two categories for the competition: one following the legally mandated requirements and one embodying advocates' aspirational goals.

Closely related to choosing mapping criteria is how the redistricting plans will be judged. Will the criteria be added together to form an overall score (an approach used by Ohio reformers)?[30] If so, the group will have to decide how such a final score will be tallied. If the highest-scoring plan will not automatically win, then we suggest approaching respected in-state experts—such as retired judges, retired politicians, reporters, and academics—to serve as judges who will evaluate how well the submissions meet the goals. In our experience, a plan can come close to maximizing all the required criteria simultaneously, but there will always be some tradeoffs among the best plans. A benefit of employing a panel of judges is they can reward a particularly innovative approach that does not necessarily fare well on other goals, such as a plan that creates an additional minority opportunity district that no one thought was possible, which is what a student team from the University of Virginia demonstrated with their Virginia state senate map.

Once it is clear what the competition is expected to achieve, participants should be informed of what information they need to submit along with their plan. If using DistrictBuilder, a competitor can share their plan publicly through the software, and the software can automatically generate statistics to score plans on the competition's criteria. Competition organizers may also wish to have participants provide a written summary of their work so that participants can describe their mapping approach and particular features of their plan they find noteworthy.

Participants

The next decision involves who will be invited to participate in the competition. Should the competition be open to everyone, just people within a state, or a specific group, such as students? If participants do not need to prove their identity, there is no way to verify in the digital age who participates. Indeed, Florida Republicans had political operatives submit maps anonymously through the state's online portal in an attempt to disguise the source of their gerrymanders.[31] As a practical matter, if participants are not verified, then the competition is open to everyone, everywhere. Indeed, we would even encourage submissions generated by automated redistricting algorithms, because having more maps helps us understand what is possible. Participants in student competitions can be verified through faculty advisors. We've found student competitions can be incorporated into class curricula that include scholarly and legal writings on redistricting, and they serve as a focal point for media coverage. There can, of course, be two or more divisions for a competition, with different participants in each division and overall winners.

A consideration for any competition is a prize or award that will induce people to participate. The award amount will depend on how much money a group can raise for their competition. A typical award structure is a couple thousand dollars for a first place prize, half that for a second place prize, and half again for a third place prize. Organizers may also consider awarding trophies or framed certificates.

Once the competition parameters have been set, an outreach plan can be implemented to recruit contestants. A competition open to the public can use advocacy groups' existing traditional and social media networks to notify people about the competition. Established grassroots groups are valuable coalition members because they have carefully cultivated extensive member networks. Media outreach should also be a part of recruitment, through opinion editorials placed in media outlets or blog posts that reporters and editorial boards can reference in their news stories and opinion pieces. Student recruitment flows through faculty, particularly in political science, geography, and computer science departments. These faculty can design classes or send out announcements to their students.

Scheduling

The work of developing a competition's timeline will vary among the states. The timeframe is bracketed by two events: the release of census population data and the government's formal adoption of a plan. As mentioned, the Census Bureau releases decennial population data in the beginning of years ending in a 1. As the appointed time approaches, the Census Bureau will post expected data release dates for each state, which in the past have been grouped weekly and prioritized by legal deadlines. To affect the redistricting process, winners must be announced before a government formally adopts its maps. States with a redistricting commission often have firm deadlines delineated in state constitutions. Some commissions may post public hearing schedules that may further help develop a competition's timeline. Legislative-led redistricting is more fluid. In all states, redistricting must be complete before primary candidate filing deadlines, so a competition timeline starts by working backward from this date.

Other key dates are when the legislature is in session and when the committees responsible for redistricting will meet. Be on guard when one party controls redistricting, because sneaky legislative parties may preemptively call for votes on surprise maps developed in secret with little or no warning, which happened in Wisconsin and forced us to abandon planned public mapping activities. Finally, student competitions should respect school calendars, noting when students will be on break. Schools do not necessarily have the same calendars, so it may be impossible to avoid scheduling a submission deadline that does not conflict with a school vacation; claims of bias from aggrieved students will follow. And, of course, if students are intended to be part of a competition, recruitment of participants through faculty outreach should occur in advance of a new school semester in case faculty wish to fit a competition into their class syllabi.

Technical details can also affect a timeline, particularly deciding which data to use. The Census Bureau provides a schedule of the dates they will release their data. Some time is needed to prepare the data and update redistricting software, perhaps a week or two depending on the software provider's capabilities. If a group does not wish to evaluate political effects of redistricting plans, the Census Bureau's population data are sufficient for a competition. Otherwise, additional work will be required to merge election and census data. Some states, such as California, Ohio, and Texas, have released redistricting databases of merged census and election data and will likely do so again. We recommend using these state-supplied databases unless there are obvious flaws with them, because a public discussion regarding data accuracy is not a productive one. To determine if and when a state will create and release a redistricting database, we recommend contacting state election officials, redistricting commission staff, or the legislative committees responsible for redistricting.

Once a schedule has been set, we recommend sticking with it—otherwise, participants may feel cheated if the rules change. That said, redistricting is a fluid process. Sometimes unexpected opportunities may arise to influence the process, perhaps by a governor or court soliciting input. If an organization has the capacity to respond, we encourage flexibility by adding to a competition while honoring the original framework. In our experience, technical issues can delay the release of the necessary redistricting data, or result in a whole new dataset being distributed midstream. These unfortunate events may need to be addressed through unavoidable schedule changes. If this happens, participants need to be notified promptly.

Media Involvement

We've alluded to some aspects of the necessity of a media plan. Announcements about the start of a competition and announcement of winners can take the form of press releases, blog posts, and opinion editorials, which in turn can garner more media coverage. A kickoff announcement event, with organizers and notable political leaders in the state who support redistricting reform, can be useful to attract attention to the competition. While a competition is in progress, reporters can interview contestants about how they are struggling to meet the competition's goals. We discovered, quite by accident, a competition importantly reframes redistricting from a dry process story, difficult for reporters to cover, to a human-interest story. Student competitions serve as useful focal points for media interviews, given that students often congregate in a computer lab as they do their work. A media plan should include connecting local reporters with their local student groups. An awards ceremony in a state capitol building, where contestants are invited to present their maps, makes great visuals for television. An awards ceremony also centrally locates organizers, contestants, and interested lawmakers for media interviews.

Funding a Competition

All of these activities require funding. A potential funding source is state-based charitable foundations, whose grant-making rules vary. The process typically begins with an individual or organization writing a letter of inquiry to a prospective foundation describing a proposed activity in two or three pages. Foundations may limit their funding to specific policy areas, often explicitly described on their website or may be inferred from published lists of funded projects. A letter of inquiry should explain how the activity achieves the foundation's goals. If interested, a foundation officer will invite an applicant to submit a full proposal with a detailed budget. Depending on the foundation's rules and the amount of money requested, the review may be decided in an expedited process or it may require board approval. Foundation boards do not meet often, so a decision may be delayed if a proposal requiring board approval is not submitted on the board's schedule.

Funding from private donors can come more quickly because it may not require a formal proposal and review process, but obtaining money through this route is the culmination of cultivating individuals through personal connections.

Staffing

Finally, a competition needs staff to organize it. Someone will need to develop the strategic plan, secure funding, conduct outreach to media and potential contestants, answer questions from participants, and organize judging and events. A single person could do all of these activities, but we've found that a two-person team (at least) works best, particularly to manage a competition during crunch time, when contestants are actively drawing maps. This may mean hiring staff or using existing staff within an organization. An awards event can be a large production where volunteers may be helpful. We've found that even if a state-based group does not wish to formally be part of a coalition because they have different reform strategies, they may be willing to reach into their networks to help find volunteers.

We created a checklist in table 3.1 to assist those who wish to conduct a redistricting competition. While the checklist starts with creating a strategic plan, a redistricting competition should be thought of as a whole since developing a strategic plan outlines all the competition activities. Some decisions, like the competition rules, depend on a group's goals, which in turn affect which data one may wish to

Table 3.1. A Redistricting Competition "To Do" Checklist

Develop strategic plan	☐
Fundraising	☐
Hire staff	☐
Software and data	☐
Timeline	☐
Competition rules	☐
Recruit judges	☐
Prizes	☐
Media plan	☐
Recruit participants	☐
Judging	☐
Event planning: kickoff and awards ceremony	☐

use. The checklist is just a recommendation. We encourage intrepid organizers to be creative and take ownership of their competition to meet their advocacy goals. Crowdsourcing is one of our guiding principles, so we hope folks will be inspired to devise innovative approaches.

4

DistrictBuilder

The DistrictBuilder application is a cornerstone of the Public Mapping Project, intended to foster greater public participation and transparency in redistricting. The software we developed to achieve this goal is emblematic of current redistricting applications, so it is instructive to review what DistrictBuilder does to understand how mapping applications assist humans in drawing districts and the role they play in public mapping. Our guiding principle was to create an easy-to-use internet redistricting application that allows people to quickly get up to speed and start drawing districts, rather than spend frustrating hours installing software, configuring it, and learning how to use it. High school students, retirees, and many people in between have used our software to create perfectly legal districts, something naysayers said was impossible when we embarked upon the project.

Our aspiration to create DistrictBuilder began during a 2007 American Mathematical Society meeting in Washington, DC, where we delivered a presentation of our research on automated redistricting.[32] We concluded automation was not a viable solution to gerrymandering, as explained more fully below. After our presentation, we were approached by Daniel Goroff, professor emeritus of mathematics and economics at Claremont's Harvey Mudd College and a vice president of the Sloan Foundation, a charitable organization. He challenged us: What would you do? We responded that instead of relying on machines, we would empower humans. After all, the original meaning of the word *computer* is "one who computes" as it was applied to human computers who did tedious, repetitive calculations before the advent of machine computers. There is a good reason why we sought to engage humans: our complex brains have ways of seeing solutions to problems that might elude a machine. This is particularly true with redistricting for two reasons. First, humans often perform better than computers in processing visual information like geographic units awaiting assignment to districts. For example, a computer has a difficult time seeing how to tie geographically separated communities together, whereas humans can quickly see the problem and form a solution. Second, redistricting plans are proposals for political representation—although made in a technical form. Since there is no universally agreed-upon measure of representation, it is important for the public to be able to express proposals that reflect their conception of what *representation* means. As we told Daniel Goroff, we wanted to involve more people in the redistricting process by providing them with mapping tools and data, delivered through the internet. We believed that having more eyes on the problem would help expose policy-makers, courts, media, and the general public to a wider range of possibilities beyond the gerrymandered districts offered by political parties.

Daniel was intrigued by our answer and assisted our vision by providing support from the Sloan Foundation.[33] To create DistrictBuilder, we engaged Azavea Corporation, a Philadelphia company that applies geospatial technology for positive civic, social, and environmental impact while also conducting research.[34]

Accessing DistrictBuilder

DistrictBuilder is among the new generation of redistricting applications that are web-based, so people can immediately begin mapping without having to worry about software installation and data management. What distinguishes DistrictBuilder from other redistricting applications is that it is open-source software, which means anyone can obtain the software at no cost; in our case, from a popular internet archive known as GitHub.[35] It is distributed under an open-source license, meaning that it is available to everyone for inspection and reuse.

Indeed, Bill Morris—a Burlington, Vermont, city administrator—used DistrictBuilder for his city's redistricting in 2011. We only learned about his work when he contacted us with questions. He even did some programming to meet his specific needs, later adding his programming to the DistrictBuilder code base. This illustrates another benefit of open-source software: it is in the public domain, so the public can take ownership of it to make it better. In contrast, the public cannot inspect closed-source, proprietary systems; these programs can contain errors, usually a result of unintentional software bugs, but we cannot rule out the possibility of intentional manipulation hidden from the public. For this reason, we believe strongly that election systems—be they voting systems or redistricting systems—belong to the people and should reside in the public domain.

What follows next is an orientation of DistrictBuilder's basic features. We will likely continue to modify the software to improve users' experiences, but these core functions will remain. The description offers glimpses into redistricting complexities, how we overcome them, and how we executed the vision of crowd-sourced mapping for domestic and international use. Persons wishing to draw redistricting plans or orchestrate public mapping advocacy will find this section instructive, but if the following orientation demystifies the process in somewhat too much detail for the casual reader, feel free to skip ahead to the next section, "Why Not Automated Redistricting?"

Using DistrictBuilder

An intrepid mapper needs advanced computer skills to install DistrictBuilder directly onto his or her own computer from its source code. Therefore, our user-friendly deployment model is for a knowledgeable administrator to configure the software for others to access via web browser.

Assuming the presence of an administrator familiar with cloud computing infrastructure, we made the installation process easier by placing prebuilt instances on cloud computing sites like Amazon, which has a gentler learning curve than a bare-metal installation from source code. While the software is free, a person or organization using DistrictBuilder on the computing cloud will incur charges for server time. Monthly charges run only a few dollars for personal use. Another advantage of a cloud server is that in the case of a catastrophic success—for instance, a popular rush to map new districts—increasing server capacity to accommodate demand is easy.

Here we should mention that hosting DistrictBuilder for many simultaneous users requires a hefty server that will incur higher monthly costs, perhaps into the thousands of dollars. An organization hosting a redistricting competition or general public mapping may wish to install the software on their own servers to better manage the computing load, as there are backend tricks that can optimize performance.

Login Experience and Creating Accounts

By default, DistrictBuilder allows users to create a new account from the login page. Administrators can opt out of this setting, however, and distribute login credentials themselves. This feature accommodates organizations that wish to set up internal mapping applications.

While restricting access may seem the antithesis of our public mapping philosophy, anyone can tweak the software code to do this anyway, and there are certain use cases we wish to support, such as enabling internal sharing between state and local governments during redistricting to improve the integrity of election data. For instance, a state government might wish to draw new districts or precinct boundaries, and in this case, an inefficient option would be to purchase a separate commercial software license for each state and local redistricting effort. With DistrictBuilder, however, the state can distribute credentials and work in tandem with their localities in a shared, private setting, using the same mapping system and data.

Note that a large number of users can overwhelm a server. Therefore, DistrictBuilder puts a throttle on the number of accounts that can run simultaneously. When the limit set by an administrator is reached, users will receive a message to try back later.

Basic Features

A brief tour of DistrictBuilder provides a feel for what the current generation of redistricting software looks like and does. A user's typical mapping session begins by logging into their account, selecting a new or existing plan to work on, and then mapping. With a click of a button, the software can be displayed in English, Spanish, French, or Japanese. (We chose to implement Japanese during software development because the language reads right to left.) The internationalization features work; we have had Spanish-speaking university students in Mexico successfully use the software to draw districts.

Once logged in, users are presented with a file directory containing existing maps to edit or the option to create a new map. The administrator may provide suggested starting maps. Users can select any other map that other people have shared, which will copy the map to their account for editing. Users can also copy their plans for exploratory mapping.

To become familiar with the mapping interface, it will be helpful to walk through a real-world example. In figure 4.1, the background base map looks somewhat like what one might see in a common phone map app. Cities, roads, water, and other landmarks assist in identifying the location where users are drawing districts. We use open-source base maps in this example, but there are options to use proprietary base maps, too, even including satellite imagery. In this case, these

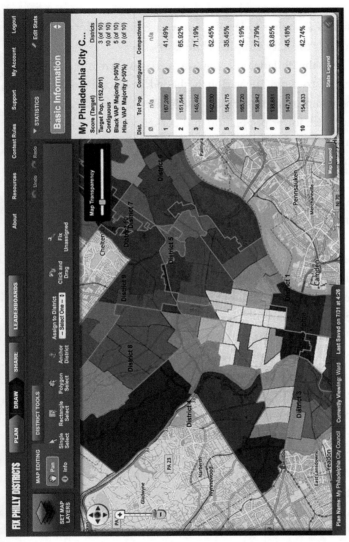

Figure 4.1. DistrictBuilder Philadelphia deployment

visual clues help us identify that we are drawing council districts for the City of Philadelphia.

Atop the Philadelphia map we overlay information needed for redistricting. The variously shaded, grayscale blocks represent Pennsylvania's wards, with lighter shading signifying a ward with lower population and darker colors a higher population. The shading scheme also tells us about each district's total population (we will explain the colors in a moment). It is possible to change what the shading signifies, however, to instead provide information about an area's racial, ethnic, or partisan composition.

Not apparent in the static figure 4.1 is a tool that allows users to zoom in and out. Users don't need to select different geographies to work with; simply zooming in and out presents logical choices. When a user zooms in, smaller pieces of geography become visible, allowing that user to work with voting precincts or even individual census blocks. Besides simplifying the user experience in an intuitive manner, this feature is incredibly important from a technical standpoint. A typical state has over a hundred thousand census blocks; displaying all of them while viewing a statewide map would place terrible strain on the server, require pushing a lot of data through the internet, and diminish the software's performance. Trimming the data to match the zoom level helps manage this performance challenge.

Meeting Legal Requirements

Redistricting plans must comply with federal and state requirements. Online resources like the Brennan Center's *A Citizen's Guide to Redistricting* and the National Conference of State Legislatures' *Redistricting Law* series are good primers on the legal intricacies. In a nutshell, federal law requires that districts have equal population, and that the task of drawing districts should ensure minorities an opportunity to elect a candidate of their choice in compliance with the Voting Rights Act and the 14th Amendment. Requirements vary by state, and sometimes even by congressional and state legislative district within the same state. Common requirements include contiguity; compactness; respecting existing political boundaries such as counties and townships; respecting communities of interest; respecting geographic features; continuity of the territory in the old and new districts, to the extent that it is possible; and even compatibility with political goals such political fairness and competitive districts.

DistrictBuilder has features that assist map drawers to achieve legal goals like these. In our example, an intrepid mapper's Philadelphia's city council districts overlay the color-coded wards. These districts are represented by gold boundaries and gold-, blue-, and clear-filled areas on our map, helping users achieve the first important federal requirement: equal population districts. The ideal target population for a district is calculated simply by dividing the population of a state or locality by the number of its districts. Blue-colored districts fall short of the ideal target population for population equality, gold-colored districts go over the target, and clear districts meet it.

The side panel on the right can display any measurable statistic about districts. Some merely add up numbers, such as districts' total or voting-age population broken down by race, ethnicity, and various election results to measure partisan leaning. Some statistics relate to districts' geography, such as whether a district is contiguous (all parts connect), district compactness (measured in different ways), how many local political boundaries are split by districts, and even the travel time across a district, which is a consideration for Mexico's federal districts.

In figure 4.1, the side panel displays districts' total population, with colored context clues for over- and under-populated districts; a checkmark indicates whether a district is contiguous (green) or not (red), and one of many available compactness measures. A pull-down menu allows users to display other preset statistics configured by an administrator, as well as a user-defined custom set of statistics.

Drawing Maps

To do mapping, a user first selects geography to assign to a district. The visual cues like color-coding and shading will suggest good pieces of geography to add to a district. A person can point and click to select a single piece of geography or use a lasso tool to select several. Once the geography is chosen, it can be grabbed, dragged, and dropped into the desired district, which assigns it to that district. This workflow functions best when editing adjoining districts to balance population. Users can also choose to immediately assign any selected geography to a specific district without dragging and dropping, which is useful when building a new district. Of course, there is an "undo" button to walk back mistakes.

An important innovation of DistrictBuilder is it enables crowd-sourced redistricting. Individuals and organizations no longer need to work independently and in isolation on their own machines. A central web server can simultaneously support several users. People can work on their districts in private, and when they are ready, share their maps publicly with others. They can copy and paste districts from any shared map into their working plan. In this way, people can work together to improve upon others' ideas.

Sharing Maps

Most important, users can share their work. Features allow the import and export of redistricting plans in commonly used data formats. Importing is useful when a government or organization releases a plan for public consumption, and exporting is useful to submit plans to governments.

Web links are generated for specific maps, which can be incorporated into news stories or social media. These links are accessed through an anonymous login that allows people to see but not edit the map. This serves two important purposes. First, people do not need to create an account to view a map. Second, stripping down the mapping interface lessens the server load, which improves users' experience.

Once created, all districts and entire plans can be scored by how well they meet various criteria. DistrictBuilder can rank shared plans on leaderboards, which list the plans that have the highest score on criteria such as district compactness, splits of local community boundaries, political fairness, and many other district and plan metrics. These individual scores can be combined into an overall score that is a weighted composite of different measures—something Mexico does formally as part of their redistricting process, and what Ohio reformers did as part of a recent redistricting competition.

Data

Redistricting software cannot work without data. In the information age it is easy to assume that data are readily available, but this has not been entirely true for redistricting.

The Census Bureau publicly releases population and geo-spatial data, the most basic necessities for drawing districts. Most state governments have not made the election data necessary, even if politicians use these data to assess the consequences of moving district boundaries to add or subtract a partisan-leaning community from their district. Keeping such information private prevents the public from doing the same evaluation, so the public cannot know to what degree a proposed redistricting plan is a gerrymander.

Augmenting census data with election data is costly, as it requires collecting both election boundaries and election results and marrying these data to census data. A few states, such as California, Hawaii, Louisiana, Michigan, Minnesota, North Carolina, Oklahoma, Texas, Utah, and Wisconsin, maintain websites where they provide election boundaries and election results for every election on a statewide basis. Sometimes states will release redistricting databases of merged election and census data in the midst of redistricting, such as in Ohio's case. In other states, these data must be collected from localities, which can be a time-consuming process; many localities do not post their data online in accessible formats, some local election officials do not respond, or they charge for their data.

Creating redistricting databases is also possible using an alternative source of data, if a given state does not release election boundary data. In advance of the decennial census, in a year ending in a 7 or 8, the Census Bureau requests political boundary lines from states and localities in what is known as Phase 2 of the Redistricting Data Program.[36] These boundaries include what the Census Bureau calls Voting Tabulation Districts, or VTDs, which is their generic name for precinct, ward, and election district boundaries. Nearly all states participate fully in Phase 2, although in the past a few did not participate at all or provided only partial data. The availability of these data make it easier to augment census data with election data circa a year ending in 8. A catch is that some localities—primarily larger ones—continuously change election boundary lines so there is no absolute guarantee that the Census Bureau's VTD boundaries correspond with the actual boundaries used in an election. Accounting for these changes can still be tedious work.

Without diving too far into the weeds, this data work is fraught with further complexities. Briefly, one issue is how to account for election results that some states and localities do not report by precinct, such as early voting results reported only for entire counties. Another is how to merge together census and precinct data when the boundaries do not perfectly coincide with one another. We describe methodologies on how to resolve these issues elsewhere.[37] We, and other organizations, are working to collect and disseminate publicly these election data in advance of the 2020 round of redistricting.

Some state governments do this data work themselves and release a merged census and election database during redistricting. In addition to the states that continually release election boundary and results data, Arizona, Colorado, Florida, and Ohio released these databases in prior rounds of redistricting. If a state releases such a database, we recommend using it rather than duplicating a significant amount of work. The adage of "trust, but verify" applies. In the midst of the Ohio redistricting competition, the DistrictBuilder software experienced what looked to be a software bug. After frantic days of troubleshooting, Azavea discovered that the Ohio database had geographic errors that caused the software to seize up. After we notified the state, they issued a new database that still had errors. The third time was the charm, but we were delayed for weeks—at considerable expense—by an error that people wrongly associated with DistrictBuilder when the state's data were to blame.

Why Not Automated Redistricting?

Our DistrictBuilder software description raises a natural question: Why not just let computers do redistricting all and take the grubby self-dealing humans out of the equation? You're not alone in asking this question. As then-governor Ronald Reagan stated, "There is only one way to do reapportionment—feed into the computer all the factors except political registration."[38] Many others have subsequently supported this viewpoint. So, why not just let machines do the job?

The short answer why we shouldn't just hand over redistricting to computers is that humans program computers. A programmer is faced with many choices when creating an algorithm that automatically draws districts. These choices might unintentionally or intentionally bias a computer to select a particular type of redistricting plan, thereby substituting human gerrymandering for machine gerrymandering. Furthermore, these programming choices often embed interpretations of representational values, such as fairness and protection of communities of interest, that should emerge as the *result* of the redistricting process—not be defined by it.

The long answer is that programming computers to do redistricting is surprisingly really hard. James Weaver and Sidney Hess, the Delaware advocates who created the first automated redistricting application in the early 1960s, understood this limitation because they approached the problem from an operations sciences background. In this field, businesses have high demand for mathematical solutions to similar problems that cost companies substantial amounts of money.[39] They did not completely dismiss a role for computers; after all, they wrote the first automated redistricting algorithm. Stuart Nagel, who developed an algorithm soon after, observed that an automated redistricting algorithm is useful in "testing some policy proposals."[40] By virtue of being able to generate a large number of plans quickly, computers help inform us about the available choices. Curiously, when it comes to redistricting, the wheel is constantly being reinvented by contemporary scholars who rediscover some of the lessons of these early efforts.[41]

Redistricting is a mathematically hard problem because there is a staggeringly large number of redistricting plans. A modest-sized state may have a hundred thousand census blocks, which might be partitioned into five or six congressional districts or fifty or more state legislative districts. To get an idea of why there are so many redistricting plans, imagine flipping a coin and noting whether it comes up heads or tails. Now imagine flipping the coin one hundred thousand times, with each sequence of heads and tails representing a unique redistricting plan. The number of possible combinations of heads and tails boggles the mind. There are more possible redistricting plans than quarks in the universe, and if every computer on Earth were set to the task of redistricting, the sun would engulf the Earth before the computers could draw all the feasible plans.

A proponent of automated redistricting might counter that a computer need not find all the redistricting plans. To work well it needs only to find the best redistricting plan, or else randomly sample redistricting plans. A problem with this approach is that a computer cannot be simply programmed to choose the best plan or an unbiased random selection of plans. Thinking back to our coin-flipping exercise, it would be tempting to think that a computer algorithm could just virtually flip a coin a hundred thousand times to produce a legal redistricting plan. Computers complete repetitive tasks very quickly. It turns out this approach is terribly inefficient in finding legal redistricting plans. Our sequence of coin flips would technically be a redistricting plan, but it might not be a legal redistricting plan because it gives too much or too little population to a district, creates noncontiguous districts, violates the Voting Rights Act or other state constitutional or statutory requirements, and so on. The problem is that we don't know which sequence of coin flips will result in a legal plan until we start flipping the coin. Like the proverbial monkeys banging on typewriters in search of Shakespeare's complete works, an incredibly large number of unsuccessful coin flips is needed to draw a single legal redistricting plan.

Proponents of automated redistricting get around this complexity problem in two ways. Their first approach simplifies the problem. Instead of drawing districts out of census blocks, they draw them out of larger voting precincts. This reduces the number of geographic units to assign from the hundreds of thousands to a few thousand. Simplification makes the problem more computationally manageable, but this simplification produces districts that are not legal, most obviously because combinations of voting precincts rarely produce districts with equal population.

Even by reducing the number of units to assign to districts, redistricting is still a staggeringly difficult problem such that a computer still cannot efficiently search for the best plan or randomly sample with as few as forty geographic units to assign to districts. A second simplification uses a heuristic to draw redistricting plans. Heuristics are rules to solve problems, such as when in a maze, always turning right when hitting a wall before proceeding forward again will eventually get you to the exit. The problem with applying heuristics to very complex problems is they are not guaranteed to find good solutions. Trapped in a really large maze, one might die before exiting if constrained to only making right turns. Automated redistricting algorithms typically use variants of the following heuristic, first implemented in the 1960s:

Step 1. Select a random census block (or precinct).

Step 2. Randomly assign adjacent census blocks until a legal district is created. Repeat Step 1 and Step 2 as needed to create an entire redistricting plan.

Step 3. Make random trades of census blocks between adjacent districts until a legal (or optimal plan) is created.

Surprisingly, doing random things does not guarantee random results. A frequent heuristic is the random assignment of adjacent census blocks to build districts (Step 2). This tends to, but does not always, favor the creation of districts that are centrally clustered over those that are dispersed. Some may view this as a feature, not a bug, but it means that this heuristic will not actually search the space of all legal redistricting plans, potentially missing some that perform better on the goals one may care about. For example, such automated algorithms have trouble creating voting rights districts, which sometimes require tying together nonadjacent communities of color.

In a third step, an automated algorithm trades geography in pursuit of creating an optimal plan. There are subtle but important complications to this approach. Computers can only be programmed with measurable goals. A particularly problematic goal is respecting communities of interest, which twenty-four states require for state legislative redistricting and thirteen for congressional redistricting.[42]

There is no agreed-upon definition for communities of interest, so this criterion typically devolves into vague impressions of what constitutes a community by those conducting redistricting. Even when a goal can be measured, there must be agreement on how to measure it. One group of scholars finds there are over one hundred different ways to measure district compactness.[43] These various measures might examine a district's perimeter, area, convexity, and the location of its population, or take into account geographic barriers like water. Suppose that a decision can't be made on a single measure, and instead, more than one will be used. How does one combine them into a single overall measure? A simple average might make sense, but the measures might not be calculated on the same scale. This is certainly a problem if we incorporate goals other than compactness into a redistricting authority's decision-making process, such as population equality, the number of times districts split local political boundaries, and so on.

Moreover, selecting the "optimal" redistricting plan inevitably requires making decisions about how different representational values should be balanced. This is true in practice, and even in theory.[44] That is, it is impossible to simultaneously maximize competitiveness, partisan unbiasedness, communities of interest, and other desirable criteria—even when we agree on how to quantitatively measure these. Purely automated systems preempt human judgment about how to balance legitimate goals.

Perhaps one day someone will create, in the limited time available during a redistricting period, an automated redistricting algorithm that works well, draws legal districts respecting all required criteria, and can draw districts in an unbiased manner that reflects with fidelity whatever representational values the public wishes to consider. That day is not today, and given what we know about the mathematical complexity of the problems and limits of computers, such a program may not be designed in our lifetimes. Suppose it was, however—what then? Automated redistricting algorithms create samples of redistricting plans that vary across the goal one cares about. An important public policy matter like redistricting should not be a crapshoot. Human intervention is needed to make a choice among all proposed maps, be they by machine or human.

Man versus Machine: Why Not Both?

Our critique of automated redistricting should not be interpreted as a wholesale rejection of the approach. We believe automated algorithms can serve an important function to quickly develop policy alternatives for consideration, along with maps created by humans.

Mexico's use of automated redistricting illustrates both the promise and potential pitfalls in automation. Mexico's national election management board has required automation as a step in past redistricting processes for the country's single-member, lower-chamber districts.[45] Alejandro Trelles, a public mapping collaborator at Brandeis University, was formerly a staff member of Mexico's redistricting commission, what is now known as Instituto Nacional Electoral, or INE (formerly known as Instituto Federal Electoral, or IFE). Alejandro connected us to his former colleagues who have considered using DistrictBuilder as a part of the INE's official public outreach. Our communications led to access to the internal INE plans and data produced during a prior redistricting.

Mexico's redistricting process starts with an INE committee defining a set of measurable criteria to apply to districts. These criteria include population equality, compactness, respecting municipal boundaries, and minimizing travel distance across districts.[46] (DistrictBuilder can produce statistics for all these criteria.) The committee then assigns weights to these components to develop an overall score for each redistricting plan. INE then employs an optimization algorithm to draw federal districts for each of Mexico's thirty-two states. After the computer produces districts, the committee members, who are delegates of the political parties, can offer alternative plans. In the majority of states, committee members' counterproposals scored higher than those produced by a computer. Indeed, in 2013, humans offered counterproposals that scored much better than the computer-generated plans in the states of Hidalgo, Puebla, and San Luis Potosí.

Automation plays an important role in Mexico's process insofar as it constrains the choices available to the political parties. They have to play a game of beat-the-machine by producing plans that score better than the basel ine generated by the automated algorithm. This means a proposed plan must fare better on some combination of population equality, compactness, respecting municipal boundaries, and minimizing travel distance across districts. If a political party can do so, then their counterproposal may be considered for adoption by the redistricting committee. A drawback of this approach is the proverbial dog that did not bark. There is no incentive for a political party to offer a plan that makes them worse off. This may be mitigated by the involvement of other political parties, but not all parties have the same capacity to draw maps. We noticed certain larger parties making counterproposals more frequently.

Another innovative facet of Mexico's redistricting is computer-assisted design. The political parties' counter proposals accepted by the INE committee are fed into the computer and the optimization algorithm is run again to see if the computer can devise yet a better solution. In some states the computer algorithm did so, and humans were yet again able to beat the computer in some of their final counterproposals. We built similar rudimentary computer-assisted design features into DistrictBuilder. A tool identifies all the unassigned geography and helps users find these slivers of land, such as a stray census block located in a stream or road median. This can be a tedious-but-important task, because a plan that does not assign all geography to a district is not a legal plan. A completion tool automatically assigns these orphaned pieces to the nearest district.

We believe this automation approach can be improved upon using a process similar to Mexico and creating more sophisticated optimization algorithms. In this way, humans and computers can together search for the best possible plans. However, given the complexity of the redistricting problem, and given the current limits of computers, we can never know for sure whether we have found the absolute best plan. Still, slight deviations from the ideal is far better than what many states have today.

5

Public Mapping and Redistricting Reform

While we have contributed to and learned much about how to do public mapping, we have used the maps drawn by the public to discover even more about redistricting. The public approaches redistricting from a perspective fundamentally different from that of politicians. Redistricting plans produced by the public, compared to plans adopted by redistricting authorities, are generally more politically fair, have more competitive districts, have at least the same number or more voting rights districts, are more compact, and adhere more closely to existing political boundaries. Indeed, the public's plans can do all of these things better than politicians' maps, simultaneously.

How is this possible? When politicians gerrymander, they are not particularly interested in achieving any goal other than political advantage, either by personally crafting a single district to help win a future election or through an entire plan to assist their political party in a bid to control a legislature. Politicians often give only lip service to compactness, respecting local political boundaries, increasing minority representation, and other legitimate state goals. In contrast, the public is more likely to favor other goals.

Importantly, more of what the good-government advocates want can be achieved without imposing on voting rights districts. The voting rights community has been wary of the reform community's goals, particularly the goal to promote competitive districts. Minority voting rights districts are drawn to empower a minority community by giving them an opportunity to elect a candidate of their choice. The voting rights community fears that the hard-fought gains in representation they have made will be jeopardized if their districts are made more competitive. This fear is misplaced. First, as a legal matter, the federal Voting Rights Act takes precedence over all state requirements. Second, as a practical matter, politicians' maps are such extreme gerrymanders that the voting rights and reform communities are in the unusual position of being able to have their cake and eat it, too. The public has shown it is possible to draw plans that retain the same number of minority opportunity districts and increase the number of competitive districts. Indeed, in some cases it is even possible to increase the number of minority opportunity districts beyond what was previously understood to be possible. Virginia student competition maps showed how to increase minority representation in the state senate and congress, and a Florida League of Women Voters' plan showed how to increase minority representation in Congress.

The Benefits of Public Mapping

Amanda Holt, a Pennsylvania public mapping hero, exemplifies how politicians' mapping priorities conflict with the public's. In 2011, she was a piano teacher and local Republican committeewoman, and she decided that she could draw better state legislative districts than the state's redistricting commission (a political creature headed by elected officials). Using Dave's Redistricting App, she produced maps in fuller compliance with Article II, Section 16 of Pennsylvania's constitution, which requires compactness and says, "Unless absolutely necessary no county, city, incorporated town, borough, township or ward shall be divided in forming either a senatorial or representative district." With these maps, she testified before the commission.[47] When the commission adopted what she considered to be a gerrymander that violated the constitution, she sued. Upon considering her maps, along with other evidence and testimony, the Pennsylvania Supreme Court ruled in her favor in the case *Holt v. 2011 Legislative Apportionment Commission*, threw out the old districts, and ordered the state to produce new districts in compliance with the state constitution.[48]

Amanda Holt has the highest profile among the many public mapping heroes who drew legal redistricting plans. Merely creating these maps was a significant accomplishment, since naysayers said that only redistricting consultants had the expertise to draw legal plans. To illustrate how the public's approach to redistricting differs from that of politicians, we compare Florida, Ohio, and Virginia congressional plans drawn by the public with the redistricting plan adopted by the legislature. We analyze only plans that we believe to be legal, in that they are equal in population, contiguous, and have the same number of voting rights districts as the prior map.

Most public congressional redistricting plans we analyze have *de minimus* population deviations of no more than one person between the largest and smallest district. We do consider some plans with deviations of no more than 1 *percent* from the largest to smallest district. The latter plans may be legal, as the federal courts permit states to have up to a 1 percent deviation for congressional districts if there is a legitimate state interest. We consider plans with the same number of minority opportunity districts as the prior congressional plan, and each district must have no less a percentage of the minority voting-age population than the smallest value found in the prior plan as measured with 2000 Census population data.[49] We have not conducted exhaustive racial voting analyses to verify that these maps would be in full compliance with the Voting Rights Act. However, we feel the public's maps drawn to these standards would reasonably be considered legal.

We choose Florida, Ohio, and Virginia because these three states are relatively large battleground states where gerrymandering is most potent. If Democrats controlled Idaho's redistricting process, no legal plan exists that would allow them to reliably control one of this strongly Republican state's two congressional districts. Republicans controlled Florida, Ohio, and Virginia's redistricting, and all three states are considered examples of the party's gerrymandering prowess.[50]

We investigated previously public maps created in these three states and review our prior analyses here, particularly with respect to the trade-off between compactness and political fairness.[51] These three goals illustrate the extent to which politicians are willing to maximize partisan advantage and personal electoral safety, even to the detriment of compactness. In our prior writing, we demonstrated that these political goals conflict sharply with the goals of respecting local political boundaries and preserving minority representation. The choice of compactness, in particular, also addresses conventional wisdom among political pundits and political scientists that Democrats gerrymander themselves by living in urban centers.[52] The existence of politically fair redistricting plans that are also highly compact dispels this belief.

For the sake of parsimony, we evaluate only one compactness measure known as the Schwartzberg measure. Because states have different geographies that affect compactness—natural and local political boundaries—we average the Schwartzberg measure across districts and normalize the measures across states so they are roughly on the same scale. To measure partisan fairness and the number of competitive districts, we used the 2008 normalized two-party presidential vote.[53] For partisan fairness, we consider a district to be Democratic-leaning if it has a two-party vote share greater than 50 percent. For competitiveness, we consider a district to be competitive if the two-party vote share lies between 45 and 55 percent.[54]

We compare the adopted redistricting plan with public plans in Florida, Ohio, and Virginia. For Florida, we present public plans submitted to the legislature. We do not know the origin of these plans. At least some were likely generated using the legislature's homegrown online mapping tools. Others may have been created using commercial software, particularly the (unknown to us) plans drawn by Republican consultants and submitted by third parties. The Ohio and Virginia public plans were drawn by redistricting competition contestants using the DistrictBuilder software. Ohio's competition was open to the general public, while the Virginia competition was open only to Virginia university and college students. Both competitions had compactness, partisan fairness, and competitive districts among their judging criteria, which affected the range of public plans because contestants drew plans to achieve these and other goals.

Partisan Fairness

Our analysis of the trade-off between political fairness and compactness is presented in figure 5.1. A "fair" plan might be where half of the districts lean toward the Democratic Party. Florida has twenty-seven districts, so a fair map has thirteen or fourteen Democratic-leaning districts. Ohio has sixteen districts, so a fair map has eight Democratic-leaning districts. Virginia has thirteen districts, so a fair map has six or seven Democratic-leaning districts.

The dark triangles in the figure represent where an adopted plan falls on political fairness and compactness. In all three states, the adopted plans are objectively unfair. In Florida there are only ten of twenty-seven Democratic-leaning districts, in Ohio there are five of sixteen, and in Virginia there are four of thirteen. The public maps tend to score higher for fairness. There are several that have a number of Democratic-leaning districts to be considered a fair division of the state. Most score better on fairness than the adopted plan, except for a few that score worse. A similar dynamic is present with compactness. In Ohio and Virginia, the adopted plan is much less compact than most of the public plans. In Florida, the adopted plan is just less compact than the median public plan.

Also of importance in figure 5.1 is the two-dimensional comparison of partisan fairness and compactness. There clearly exist numerous plans that are simultaneously more

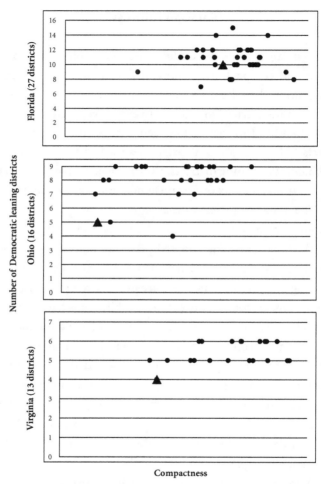

Figure 5.1 Partisan fairness versus compactness of the adopted congressional plan (triangle) and public plans (circles) in Florida, Ohio, and Virginia

politically fair and compact than the adopted plan. A fair and compact map is possible. Indeed, in subsequent litigation, a map from the Florida League of Women Voters that is politically fair and more compact than the adopted plan was ordered to be put into effect by a state court in *Romo v. Detzner*, a lawsuit challenging Florida's congressional districts on state constitutional grounds. The notion that Democrats gerrymander themselves by where they live, and that as a consequence a fair congressional map is impossible to draw in these states, is laid to rest by the existence of these alternative maps.

Competitive Districts

We observe a similar dynamic with the number of competitive districts, as presented in figure 5.2. In Florida and Ohio, the adopted plan typically fares poorly with respect to both the number of competitive districts and compactness, suggesting that like partisan fairness, geography is not limiting the number of competitive districts in these states.

This pattern does not hold well for Virginia. The adopted plan fares well on the number of competitive districts, with only a single public map having more such districts. However, as we've already seen with partisan fairness, the adopted plan fares poorly on compactness compared to the public

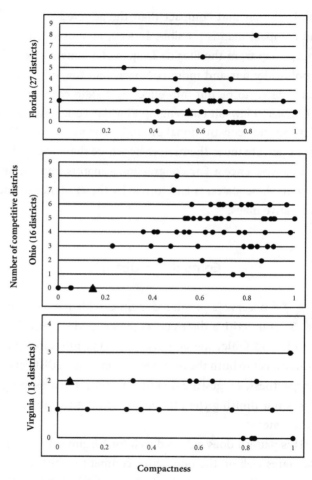

Figure 5.2 District competition versus compactness of the adopted congressional plan (triangle) and public plans (circles) in Florida, Ohio, and Virginia

maps. When we take into account the partisan fairness analysis, we surmise Virginia Republicans sought to spread their supporters across districts in order to have more districts that leaned toward their party. Indeed, when we investigate further, we observe that the range that defines a competitive district matters, as the competitive districts are just within the cusp of the competitiveness range, with districts that score slightly higher than 45 percent Democratic performance.

Public Mapping as a Redistricting Reform Strategy

We believe public mapping should be a component of redistricting reform. Redistricting is an astoundingly complex problem that benefits from having more maps to help inform the range of possible policy choices. Furthermore, we cannot trust politicians to be good actors. They will subvert legitimate redistricting goals to gerrymander for political and personal gain. At least some members of the public are removed from illicit intent, and will thus draw redistricting plans that cover more of the range of policy choices than if politicians alone drew districts.

Our proposal is not new. Fifty years ago, Stuart Nagel astutely observed that automated redistricting algorithms could help inform the public policy options.[55] We suggest rather than relying solely on machines, the solution should invoke the human brain's capacity for insight and imagination.

Our solution has a modern twist, in that technological innovations make it possible to empower people, with minimal training, to draw legal redistricting plans.

We see public mapping fitting in at two important and intertwined stages of the redistricting process. First, we believe redistricting authorities should accept, consider, and be responsive to redistricting plans created by the public. Second, we believe that public mapping can help inform the courts about the intent of a redistricting authority. If a legislature or commission knows of a map that better satisfies federal and state requirements, but selects a different plan, then something other than legal compliance motivated the adoption of a map. Here, public mapping helps inform courts about the character of the paths not taken and why a redistricting authority chose one path over others. Additional maps drawn by the public provide more ways to evaluate an adopted plan.

Recommendations

Our public mapping experiences demonstrate that the public can draw legal redistricting plans and express their representational needs to a redistricting authority. This is most vividly illustrated in the Minneapolis city council redistricting, which is the motivating example for this book. Community organizations used DistrictBuilder to propose districts for the consideration of their city's redistricting group, which in turn liked the ideas and incorporated them into their adopted redistricting plan. The Minneapolis experience goes beyond being a proof of concept, showing that the public can draw legitimate maps and be full partners in the redistricting process—that is, if a redistricting authority is willing to listen and respond. We thus make the following recommendations as part of redistricting reform.

First, we recommend transparency. The redistricting authority should make available to the public the data they are using to draw districts, particularly in any circumstance where a redistricting authority augments or modifies census data. In the pursuit of full replicability, the source and the actual data used to supplement census data will be made public. Most frequently, we have in mind the situation where a redistricting authority adds election results to census data. However, transparency can extend to other information used in redistricting, such as states that modify census population counts to reallocate felony prisoners to their home locations, communities of interest (as defined by a redistricting authority) that will be taken into account during the process, and so on. Ideally, transparency extends to mapping software, enabling the public to have access to the same software, loaded with the same data, as used by the redistricting authority. Redistricting software should be open-source so that interested parties can verify the correctness of the program's code, such that there are no bugs, unintentional or intentional, hiding therein.

Second, we recommend public input. If a tree falls in the woods and no one is there to hear it, does it make a sound? This is also true for redistricting. A legislature or commission needs to listen to the public in order for public mapping to affect the process. A formal public comment period is required for the Arizona Independent Redistricting Commission, because the state constitution stipulates that it must "advertise a draft map of congressional districts and a draft map of legislative districts to the public for comment, which comment shall be taken for at least thirty days."[56] In practice, the AIRC has accepted public comment at meetings held throughout the redistricting process. Ohio adopted redistricting reform also explicitly requiring public comment, starting in 2021: "Before adopting, but after introducing, a proposed plan, the commission shall conduct a minimum of three public hearings across the state to present the proposed plan and shall seek public input regarding the proposed plan."[57] Enshrining participation into a constitution assures it will occur, but such a step is not necessary. Commissions and legislatures may solicit public comment through statutes and legislative resolutions. A study by Peter Miller and Bernard Grofman of public hearings in nine Western states (including Arizona) identified 209 meetings where a legislature or commission solicited public comment on proposed congressional draft maps.[58]

Third and relatedly, we recommend that public input be solicited in a way that supports litigation, if needed. If politicians do not produce a redistricting plan that meets the legal requirements, they must be held to account. The Pennsylvania litigation is exemplary in this regard—the Pennsylvania Supreme Court found a state constitutional violation based, in part, on Amanda Holt's map that respected the state constitution better than the plan adopted by the state's commission. We believe that a litigation strategy involving public mapping is most potent when the legislature is aware of the public's alternatives during the redistricting process. Our prior analysis demonstrates that the public can produce legal redistricting plans that exceed adopted redistricting plans on mandated requirements. When public maps are a part of the deliberation process, politicians cannot feign ignorance of better legal plans. We thus recommend that a reform strategy include public input not only to facilitate a responsive legislature or commission, but also to lay down markers that force politicians to respect legal requirements at least as well as the public maps do, else their gerrymanders will be challenged in court.

Fourth, we recommend responsiveness. Once a redistricting authority listens to public input they should take reasonable action to address it. The evidence to this effect is promising, but mixed. The study of the Western states finds commissions or legislatures incorporated feasible public comments into revisions of draft maps about half of the time. These public comments were primarily of the caliber of "citizens bringing local knowledge to bear and reflecting local concerns."[59] A potential downside is that politicians have a choice of which comments they choose to implement. Legislatures were most responsive to comments asking to reverse changes made to the map used in the prior decade, suggesting "legislatures are likely to maintain district lines where possible."[60] A twisted scenario unfolded in Florida, where the Republican Party subverted the public input process by having their pawns submit maps drawn by Republican consultants for consideration by the legislature, which unsurprisingly found these proposed maps pleasing.[61]

Fifth, we recommend justification. When a redistricting authority adopts a map to be used in future elections, it should justify how districts were designed. If a district boundary line is to be drawn—either keeping a community intact or dividing it—the redistricting authority should explain its rationale. This is particularly important where redistricting authorities, particularly legislatures, exert what is known as legislative privilege, which prevents outsiders from knowing the content of internal deliberations. When decision making is enshrined in the public record, an objective assessment of a redistricting authority's approach can be made, particularly if there exist public maps that demonstrate better approaches to achieve the same stated goals.

In cases where a redistricting commission receives a large volume of public comments, possibly there is too much of a good thing. Redistricting happens on a compressed time schedule. A redistricting authority can only listen to and consider a finite amount of public input before the clock runs out and they need to take action. A redistricting authority does not have unlimited resources to manage many comments and map suggestions. In the extreme, we would not expect humans to be capable of examining the merits of millions of redistricting plans generated by a computer algorithm. As interest in redistricting and public mapping continues to increase, sensible management of public comments should occur. Perhaps public map submissions should be accompanied by a written justification, similar to what we desire from redistricting authorities; such a requirement may help draw attention to the serious and thoughtful proposals worthy of consideration. Still, the difficulty that arose when approximately 20,000 public comments were submitted to California's commission highlights a need for better methods of creating a usable summary of a large number of such comments.

Sixth, we recommend that redistricting authority rest in structurally independent redistricting commissions.[62] In particular, commissions should not be forced to follow automatic quantitative criteria—instead they should be authorized to make fair judgments using all socially relevant information. Further, redistricting commissions must have funding free from legislative manipulation to set up permanent staff to provide expertise, analyze public input, and maintain institutional records. And, once redistricting plans are finalized by commissions, the plans should not be subject to legislative veto or modification.

Conclusion

Our conception of public mapping is a natural extension of the democratic ideal of self-governance, whereby the government is responsive to the will of the people. Normally, the public pushes and pulls the levers of democracy through their participation in elections. When elected representatives subvert the electoral machinery so as to perpetuate their continued election, the will of the people is subverted and a democracy slides toward despotism. Active public participation in government policy making serves as a check on those in power. In the abstract, our approach is not novel. John Stuart Mill argued in his 1859 essay, "On Liberty," how the people can protect themselves from the government's infringement of their liberties: "It is indispensable, therefore, that the means should exist, independently of the government, of forming such ability, and furnishing it with the opportunities and experience necessary for a correct judgment of great practical affairs."

Mill's successors have implemented public participation spanning a wide range of policy areas, from coastal resource management to defense policy.[63] The public mapping project seeks to expand the range to include redistricting. Politicians have enjoyed a veil of complexity—embodied by data and software—that effectively shuts the public out of the important task of redistricting. The result has been a gerrymandered gruel offered as the only dish on the menu. But there are many more choices, practically an infinite number. Rather than accepting what politicians serve, we seek to empower the public to generate their own recipes. Through our efforts we observe that given the proper tools, even novices can create masterpieces.

The public can develop ideas that impel a response from redistricting authorities. Our greatest success occurred in Minneapolis, where local community groups used the District Builder redistricting software to express their representation needs to a local city redistricting commission. The commission adopted their ideas, and the result was the creation of districts that fostered the election of the first Somali and Latino candidates to the city council. Similar successes, perhaps with not as significant an effect, occurred in Western states during their congressional redistricting processes.[64] Redistricting authorities ignore the public at their peril, for comparison maps drawn by the public allow courts to evaluate when politicians have subverted the law for private or partisan gain. Pennsylvania politicians learned this lesson the hard way when the state Supreme Court threw out the state legislative maps, in part due to the existence of a redistricting plan created by a piano teacher.

We estimate the number of legal congressional and state legislative redistricting plans drawn by individuals or non-government organizations increased by about two orders of magnitude following the 2010 Census, compared to the previous decade. We expect the rise of public mapping to further increase after the 2020 Census. The software tools and data are more ubiquitous, state reforms have mandated that redistricting authorities listen to the public, and—compared to a decade ago—ongoing reform efforts, court actions, and larger organizations are stimulating public interest. We intend to continue our contribution to public mapping in the United States and abroad. Best of all, we know that our work can continue even without us, for our work is enshrined in open-source repositories available to all.

Notes

1   These federal criteria are population equality and the Voting Rights Act. State and local goals may include drawing compact districts, respecting local political boundaries, respecting communities of interest, maximizing continuity of representation, producing fair plans that reflect the state's partisan character, and producing competitive districts.

2   There are twenty-four states that allow persons outside the legislature to collect signatures to put a ballot question before voters for their approval. The National Conference of State Legislatures (NCSL) maintains a list of the varying ballot question rules. The list is available on the NCSL's website, accessed May 5, 2018, http://www.ncsl.org/research/elections-and-campaigns/chart-of-the-initiative-states.aspx.

3   See "Minneapolis Charter Commission" on the city's website, accessed May 22, 2018, http://www.ci.minneapolis.mn.us/charter/index.htm.

4   Justin Levitt and Michael P. McDonald, "Taking the 'Re' out of Redistricting: State Constitutional Provisions on Redistricting Timing," *Georgetown Law Review* 95, no. 4 (2007): 1247–1286.

5   Stuart S. Nagel, "Simplified Bipartisan Computer Redistricting," *Stanford Law Review* 17, no. 5 (1965): 863–869, 898.

6   See "A Review of Redistricting in Washington State" on the League of Women Voters of Washington's website, accessed May 9, 2018, https://leagueofwomenvotersofwashington.wildapricot.org/resources/Documents/Redistricting/Redistricting%20Report%20Appendices.pdf.

7   Michael P. McDonald, "A Comparative Analysis of U.S. State Redistricting Institutions," *State Politics and Policy Quarterly* 4, no. 4 (2004): 371–396.

8   Ridgeway Davis, "Connecticut," in *Reapportionment Politics: The History of Redistricting in the 50 States*, ed. Leroy Hardy, Alan Heslop, and Stuart Anderson (Beverly Hills, CA: Sage Publications, 1981).

9   James B. Weaver and Sidney W. Hess, "A Procedure for Nonpartisan Districting: Development of Computer Techniques," *Yale Law Journal* 73, no. 2 (1963): 288–308.

10   The Census Bureau released population data for selected geographic units as early as the 1890 census, but did not begin the widespread dissemination of census block data until the 1970 decennial census. See "Tracts and Block Numbering Areas" on the Census Bureau's website, accessed May 27, 2018, https://www.census.gov/history/www/programs/geography/tracts_and_block_numbering_areas.html.

11   A legal reason exists for these differing equal population standards. The courts apply different sections of the federal constitution to congressional districts than they do to other districts; they apply the Article IV, Section 4 guarantee of a republican form of government to congressional districts and the 14th Amendment's Equal Protection Clause to all other districts.

12 Micah Altman, Karin MacDonald, and Michael P. McDonald, "From Crayons to Computers: The Evolution of Computer Use in Redistricting," *Social Science Computing Review* 23, no. 2 (2005): 334–346.

13 Admittedly, this is an overgeneralization. States including Arkansas, Iowa, and West Virginia continued to draw districts out of their counties as late as the 2000s. However, today, no state uses counties or local boundaries as the basis for drawing districts.

14 Altman, MacDonald, and McDonald, "From Crayons to Computers," 337.

15 Peter Miller and Bernard Grofman, "Public Hearings and Redistricting: Evidence from the Western United States 2011–2012," *Election Law Journal* 17, no. 1 (2018): 21–38.

16 Michael P. McDonald, "Regulating Redistricting," *PS: Political Science and Politics* 40, no. 4 (2007): 675–679.

17 An archived version of the AIRC's website is available at https://www.azredistricting.org/2001/default.asp.

18 See https://www.azredistricting.org/2001/Meetings/PDF/AIRCTranscriptsPublicSession8-9-01.pdf at p. 9.

19 See ibid. at pp. 13–14.

20 See https://www.azredistricting.org/2001/Meetings/PDF/AIRCTranscriptsPublicSession7-17-01.pdf at pp. 6–9.

21 Dave's Redistricting App is available at http://gardow.com/davebradlee/redistricting/launchapp.html.

22 Information for Maptitude Online is available at https://www.caliper.com/redistricting/online_redistricting.htm. Information for Citygates' Autobound is available at http://www.citygategis.com/redistricting.

23 Accessed June 25, 2018, http://www.oakpark.com/News/Articles/11-16-2010/Lawrence-Hansen,-69,-Joyce-Foundation-vice-presiden.

24 Accessed June 25, 2018, https://www.brennancenter.org/publication/citizens-guide-redistricting.

25 Ken Clark and Roberta Voss, "Free Redistricting Tool Uses Incredible Power of 'Crowdsourcing," *Arizona Capital Times*, May 20, 2011, accessed June 25, 2018, https://azcapitoltimes.com/news/2011/05/20/free-redistricting-tool-uses-incredible-power-of-%E2%80%98crowdsourcing%E2%80%99.

26 Ken Clark, Roberta Voss, et al., "Online Tool Alters Mapping Game," *The Arizona Republic*, August 6, 2011, accessed June 25, 2018, http://archive.azcentral.com/arizonarepublic/viewpoints/articles/2011/08/06/20110806remapping-clark07.html.

27 These submissions are available on the redistricting commission's website, accessed June 25, 2018, https://www.azredistricting.org/Maps/Citizens-Submissions.asp.

28 Wayne Hanson, "Ohio Holds Public Redistricting Competition," *Government Technology*, March 20, 2009, accessed June 25, 2018, http://www.govtech.com/e-government/Ohio-Holds-Public-Redistricting-Competition.html.

29 See the following resources, accessed July 17, 2018: http://redistricting.lls.edu, https://www.brennancenter.org/analysis/50-state-guide-redistricting, and http://www.ncsl.org/research/redistricting.aspx.

30 Micah Altman and Michael P. McDonald, "Redistricting by Formula: The Case of Ohio," *American Politics Research* 46, no. 1 (2017): 103–131.

31 Marc Caputo, "Florida Senate Broke Law, Will Redraw Districts," *Politico*, July 28, 2015, accessed June 25, 2018, https://www.politico.com/story/2015/07/florida-senate-agrees-to-redraw-districts-120739.

32 Micah Altman and Michael P. McDonald, "BARD: Better Automated Redistricting," *Journal of Statistical Software* 42, no. 5 (2011): 1–28.

33   Without the Sloan Foundation's investment, we could never have developed DistrictBuilder. Other organizations subsequently contributed to the software development and data collection as well, such as the Joyce Foundation, the William Penn Foundation, the Judy Ford Wason Center for Public Policy at Christopher Newport University, and Amazon Corporation.

34   Azavea was funded through the grants we received, and further donated a considerable amount of pro bono effort to software development and maintenance. We are very thankful for the tremendous amount of work Azavea's president, Robert Cheetham, and the many skilled programmers contributed to the development of DistrictBuilder.

35   The DistrictBuilder source code is available from https://github.com/PublicMapping/DistrictBuilder.

36   See guidance for accessing data resources on the Census Bureau's website, accessed June 28, 2018, https://www.census.gov/rdo.

37   For details on the techniques to merge census and election data, see: Michael P. McDonald, "Calculating Presidential Vote in Legislative Districts," *State Politics and Policy Quarterly* 14, no. 2 (2014): 196–204; and Brian Amos, Michael P. McDonald, and Russell Watkins, "When Boundaries Collide: Constructing a Database of Election and Census Data," *Public Opinion Quarterly* 81, no. S1 (2017): 385–400.

38   Tom Goff, "Governor Urges Redistricting Plan without Partisan Politics," *Los Angeles Times*, January 21, 1972, at A3.

39   Weaver and Hess, "A Procedure for Nonpartisan Districting."

40   Nagel, "Simplified Bipartisan Computer Redistricting."

41   Bruce E. Cain, Wendy K. Tam Cho, Yan Y. Liu, and Emily R. Zhang, "A Reasonable Approach to Gerrymandering: Using Automated Plan Generation to Evaluate Redistricting Proposals," *William and Mary Law Review* 59, no. 5 (2018): 1521–1557.

42   More information available on the All About Redistricting website, accessed June 1, 2018, http://redistricting.lls.edu/where-state.php#communities.

43   Aaron Kaufman, Gary King, and Mayya Komisarchik, "How to Measure Legislative District Compactness If You Only Know It When You See It" (working paper), accessed October 27, 2017, https://gking.harvard.edu/files/gking/files/compact.pdf.

44   See the foundational work of Richard G. Niemi and John Deegan, "A Theory of Political Districting," *American Political Science Review* 72, no 4 (1978): 1304–1323.

45   Alejandro Trelles, Micah Altman, Eric Magar, and Michael P. McDonald, "Datos abiertos, transparencia y redistritación en México," *Política y Gobierno* 23, no. 2 (2016).

46   INE requires protection of indigenous populations. They do so at the stage of producing their redistricting database, by creating inviolate geographic units for indigenous communities.

47   Eric Boehm, "Piano Teacher Plays a Different Kind of Redistricting Plan," *Pennsylvania Watchdog*, September 29, 2011, accessed June 29, 2018, https://www.watchdog.org/pennsylvania/piano-teacher-plays-a-different-kind-of-redistricting-plan/article_6b3e1d8a-6d3a-5bb6-8975-028831ea5414.html.

48   *Holt v. 2011 Legislative Reapportionment Commission*, accessed June 29, 2011, https://caselaw.findlaw.com/pa-supreme-court/1593573.html.

49   All Florida plans have three minority opportunity districts, and Ohio and Virginia each had one.

50   Bill Marsh, "The Imbalance of Power," *The New York Times*, February 2, 2013, accessed July 17, 2018, https://archive.nytimes.com/www.nytimes.com/interactive/2013/02/03/sunday-review/imbalance-of-power.html?smid=fb-share.

51   Micah Altman and Michael P. McDonald, "Redistricting and Polarization," in *American Gridlock: The Sources, Character, and Impact of Political Polarization*, ed. James Thurber and Antonie Yoshinaka (Cambridge: Cambridge University Press, 2015); Micah Altman and Michael P. McDonald, "Florida Congressional Redistricting," in *Jigsaw Politics in the Sunshine State*, ed. Seth McKee (Gainesville : University Press of Florida, 2015); Altman and McDonald, "Redistricting by Formula." 103–131; Micah Altman and Michael P. McDonald, "A Half-Century of Virginia Redistricting Battles: Shifting from Rural Malapportionment to Voting Rights and Participation," *University of Richmond Law Review* 47 (2013): 771–831.

52   Jowei Chen and Jonathan Rodden, "Unintentional Gerrymandering: Political Geography and Electoral Bias in Legislatures," *Quarterly Journal of Political Science* 8, no. 3 (2014): 239–269.

53   We only consider votes for Barack Obama and John McCain and normalize the presidential vote by subtracting the national presidential margin from individual districts' vote shares, which creates a hypothetical, perfectly competitive national election where each candidate received 50 percent of the vote.

54   This competitiveness range is for illustration using an easily understood range. We have developed more sophisticated competitiveness measures in other academic and practical work; e.g., Michael P. McDonald, "Drawing the Line on District Competition," *PS: Political Science and Politics* 39, no. 1 (2006): 91–94.

55   Nagel, "Simplified Bipartisan Computer Redistricting."

56   Arizona Constitution, Article IV, Section 1, Part 1 (16).

57   Ohio Constitution. Article X1, Section 1(3)(C).

58   Miller and Grofman, "Public Hearings and Congressional Redistricting," 21–38.

59　Ibid., 30.

60　Ibid., 32.

61　Mary Ellen Klas, "Data Sleuths Decoded Florida's Redistricting Conspiracy," *Tampa Bay Times*, September 5, 2015, accessed July 2, 2018, http://www.tampabay.com/news/politics/stateroundup/ data-sleuths-decoded-floridas-redistricting-conspiracy/2244361.

62　See Micah Altman and Michael P. McDonald, "How Independent Commissions Could Use the Internet and Open Software to Maximize Transparency and Public Engagement in Redistricting," *Scholars Strategy Network*, July 14, 2014, accessed July 17, 2018, https://scholars.org/brief/how-independent-commissions-could-use-internet-and-open-software-maximize-transparency-and; and Micah Altman and Michael P. McDonald, "Redistricting Principles for the Twenty-First Century," *Case Western Reserve Law Review* 62, no. 4 (2012): 1179–1204.

63　For a review categorizing different approaches to engage the public, see Helena Catt and Michael Murphy, "What Voice for the People? Categorising Methods of Public Consultation," *Australian Journal of Political Science* 38, no. 3 (2003): 407–421.

64　Miller and Grofman, "Public Hearings and Congressional Redistricting,"

About the Authors

Micah Altman is Director of Research and Head/Scientist, Program on Information Science for the MIT Libraries, at the Massachusetts Institute of Technology. He previously served as a Non-Resident Senior Fellow at The Brookings Institution, and at Harvard University as the Associate Director of the Harvard-MIT Data Center, Archival Director of the Henry A. Murray Archive, and Senior Research Scientist in the Institute for Quantitative Social Sciences. Altman has authored over seventy articles; a half-dozen open-source software packages; and several books and monographs that correct common computational errors made across the range of social sciences, and articulate principles for data management and dissemination.

Michael P. McDonald is Associate Professor of Political Science at the University of Florida and a Non-Resident Senior Fellow at the Brookings Institution. He is a coprincipal investigator on the Public Mapping Project, a project to encourage public participation in redistricting. Widely published in scholarly journals and law reviews, he is co-author with Micah Altman and Jeff Gill of *Numerical Issues in Statistical Computing for the Social Scientist* (John Wiley) and coeditor with John Samples of *The Marketplace of Democracy: Electoral Competition and American Politics* (Brookings Institution Press).

CPSIA information can be obtained
at www.ICGtesting.com
Printed in the USA
LVHW06s1545151018
593649LV00009B/179/P